D1452153

I Killed Mom and Other Lies

A Memoir of Early Loss

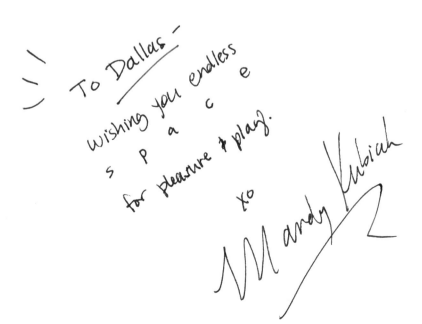

To Dallas —
wishing you endless
s p a c e
for pleasure & play.
xo
Mandy Kubicek

Also by Mandy Kubicek

My Tender Loving Self-Care Journal: The Workbook That Makes Self-Care Easy

I Killed Mom
and Other Lies

A Memoir of Early Loss

Mandy Kubicek

GLAD PANDA PRESS

Omaha, Nebraska

Published by Glad Panda Press

Glad Panda Press, P.O. Box 8228, Omaha, Nebraska 68108

I Killed Mom and Other Lies: A Memoir of Early Loss/Mandy Kubicek. —1st ed.

ISBN 978-1-7362854-1-1

Author and cover photography by Kimberly Dovi Photography

Cover design by Natalia Olbinksi

CONTENTS

Author's note

This story reflects my truth and not necessarily anyone else's.

Take, for instance, this exchange with my dad after he'd first read a draft of this book.

From across his kitchen island, I asked, "Was there anything that was… you know, inaccurate?" I was eager for a list of edits to correct my childhood chapters. His typical reading material is the Omaha World-Herald, so I assumed he'd focus on the facts.

"Sure, lots of stuff."

"Like what?"

He shrugged. "Who cares? I get it. It's how you felt. It's how you remember things."

I've combined reason and memories (mostly mine with a dash of others') with realistic details and some condensed timelines to prevent boredom. I've turned people into characters by showing you only the most relevant facets of their personalities.

Given that I've been telling everyone in my general vicinity about this book for years, I've often been asked, "When did you start?"

Who knows? I had a whiny eighty pages that felt like a draft by 2017. In early 2013 I first felt the spark that a story was being lived when I had an EMDR aha in my therapist's office and hustled home to journal about it. Well before that, a few scenes were first written as part of an essay for a high school psychology class about my mother's death.

More accurately, like all of us, I've been mentally crafting my life's stories since I learned language.

PROLOGUE

I'm over it.

My heart beat fast as I walked toward the red brick bungalow, past the sign in the yellowed lawn that read *Mourning Hope Grief Center*.

I was only seven years old when my mom died. Now in my mid-twenties, newly married with a stable job in information technology, I believed I'd made sufficient emotional progress. It was time to move forward. There was just one milestone remaining: I hadn't yet transformed my tragedy into something that might benefit others.

I admired people who hit rock bottom, rebounded, and gave back, like Oprah. I still remembered the guest speaker at my grade school who warned us in his shockingly robotic voice of the dangers of smoking cigarettes, his left hand pressing a device to his neck. Their lives seemed full of joy, despite their tragedies.

I wanted that. So, as usual, I formed a step-by-step plan to get what I wanted. I was going to volunteer with grieving children like I'd once been.

The heavy front door creaked. I felt the clash of the brisk February air against my back and, at my front, the radiator trying its best. From inside the doorway, I saw the little orange flame of a candle flickering on the end table to my right: sweet vanilla. To my left was an open walnut staircase that hugged the wall. In front of me and stretching to the right was a living room set up with a couch, a droopy loveseat, and an array of dining and folding chairs forming an approximate oval around the room. Further back, I could see a small office with piles of papers, a couple of computers, and a printer: the only sign that this home was, in fact, a business.

I was greeted with the sound of women chatting their first get-to-know-yous. Their comfortable conversation made me even more nervous. I didn't like making smalltalk with new people. I worried about what to say to sound interesting, what to ask to sound interested, and whether I'd remember their name.

This anxiety bled into existing relationships, too. I wanted intimacy but instead felt mildly disconnected from everyone in my life. I had always had the vague sense that I couldn't let people in on the whole truth of me. I may have given the impression of being an open book: telling acquaintances that I had a dead mom, talking about taboo topics like masturbation and religious hypocrisy, and sharing some of my emotional experiences with close friends. But sure it would lead to rejection, I never revealed my deepest fears and insecurities.

I chose a spot on the end of the couch, my butt landing lower than expected in the worn cushion, and set my purse on the seat beside me. The day's volunteer training at this children's grief support organization kicked off with introductions and icebreakers. Then, the instructor shared what she said would be the most important lesson of the day: how to companion. She told us that our job wasn't to fix anything. We were to walk beside. Our role was to be with someone in their pain, without urgency or judgment.

What a relief, I thought, my shoulders settling down into place. Though the approach was obvious in retrospect, I had never heard it communicated so clearly. I didn't need to make anyone feel better.

We received a handout summarizing the ways young people understand death differently at each of half a dozen age ranges. I scanned the page for the age range that included seven and skimmed the typed bullet points while the facilitator answered someone's question. At this age, I read, a child may think death is temporary (*not me*), have blunt questions about death (*not that I remember*), withdraw or be defiant (*definite yes on that first one*), blame themselves (*did I?*), and have increased fears (*yes!*) My greatest recurring fear was that my mother had become a vengeful ghost who haunted her former bedroom. My heart still pounded as I thought about rushing by that doorway as a kid.

Some volunteers, like me, came because we dealt with death ourselves as a young person. Others seemed insecure, apologetic for being there without intimately knowing our pain. The instructor reminded us that loss is more than death: it's a geographic move, an ended relationship, an identity gone. She handed blank sheets of white paper around the oval and asked us to draw a timeline of our own life and its losses.

This was an assignment I'd have no trouble completing. I'd been to so many funerals, nearly a dozen by then, that I could predict the scene.

There would be crowds of people lined up in the lobby, unpleasant instrumental music drifting in from the main room. Most would be wearing church-ready black clothes, but there'd be a few pairs of blue jeans, red Nebraska Cornhusker sweatshirts, and bright dresses mixed in. Not everyone keeps a funeral outfit clean and in her closet at all times like I did.

Some people would be in loud conversation with old friends or second cousins, enjoying the unplanned reunion. Others would stand quietly, the women expressing double the emotion as the men. Some middle-aged woman in a blazer would blot a tissue under her eyes, trying to keep the heavy black mascara in place, and I'd judge her for not just leaving it off that workday.

On a high table covered in white cotton, there would be a small rectangular guest book. It would be a many-paged lined journal with formal detailing: a leather cover, a script typeface, ornate borders. Guests would have plainly inked their names on the next available line, despite ample room to get creative.

"Any questions about the exercise before we begin?" the facilitator asked, bringing me back to the moment. We shook our heads.

I wrote fast, feeling something like pride as I penciled in the major deaths chronologically. The earliest I could remember was my maternal *Great-Grandma Rerucha,* then my first dog *Cinnamon.* Next I added *Mom. Grandpa Rerucha* died the following year*; Grandpa Partusch* died the year after that. Skipping ahead about fourteen years, I named *Uncle Chris* who had teased Bob to *put a ring on it* and lived with his cancer just long enough to see us engaged. Finally, I added *Grandma Rerucha.* My maternal grandma had just died a couple of days earlier, on my twenty-sixth birthday, from pancreatic cancer.

She had been a reserved woman, both in demeanor and appearance. She wore her short white hair in a masculine style: crispy with a sharp side part anchoring a wave. When I learned of her diagnosis, I had planned for my visit to her home by Googling *what to say to someone dying of a terminal illness.* I sat in her frozen-in-another-time kitchen, gold Tupperware canisters lined up on the counter and a laminate table that predated me, as she cried out, *Why me?* She went to Mass every Sunday. She spent summers volunteering for the church's annual White Elephant Sale. In response, I thought questions that mortified me even as they were occurring: *Why* not *you? Haven't you been miserable since Mom died?* I was genuinely surprised by how upset she was about her impending death, an aha that quickly cultivated enough compassion to abolish all other emotions. When she fearfully recounted her treatment plan, I offered one of the statements I'd memorized from the internet: *That must be so scary.* It wasn't nearly as difficult as I had expected. I mostly listened, and she wanted to talk about it.

That Christmas, knowing it would be our last with Grandma, we were especially intentional about our grandkid photo. We started this routine after years of failed attempts to convince her to participate in a full family snapshot, a tradition she refused after Mom died. This time, the men had to help Grandma get situated in the middle of her couch, and ten grandkids (every one of us except my brother) sat next to her or knelt on the floor. I was careful not to press on her oxygen cord, afraid that one absentminded misstep could take her life. The risk wasn't real, but the sweat in my palms was.

At the end, someone wheeled a hospice cot beside the bed she had shared with Grandpa until his death seventeen years before. On her last evening, I sat on the side of the bed and watched her stomach rise and fall in a steady rhythm of breath provided by machine. She looked asleep, except that her face was scrunched up in pain. Emotionally exhausted, I made my husband go home with me around dinner time. She passed away a few hours later.

"Has everyone had enough time with this exercise?"

I looked up and nodded with my peers. We went around the circle taking turns at sharing the many notches on our Loss Timelines. The distance I imagined between myself and the others when I first walked through that front door receded. One thing we all had in common was suffering.

Later, when our tour was about to begin, the volunteer coordinator took me aside. She wanted to remind me that, particularly given how recent my grandmother's death was, I didn't need to move forward with volunteering. I could reschedule my training, no questions asked.

What's the big deal? I thought, as I verbally shrugged off her offer. Her death hadn't been a surprise; she had had cancer for five months. Besides, I reasoned, I had dealt with Mom dying. This was nothing compared to that.

Upstairs, we were shown bedrooms that served as group meeting spaces. Each had a table and classroom-style chairs centered on the hardwood floor, or couches around a coffee table. There was a marker board on a wall, a few crafty bins in the corner, but mostly those rooms were for sitting and talking.

The basement, in contrast, was set up for the littlest kids with at least three distinct spaces. There was a place to sit in a circle on the floor and participate as a facilitated discussion group. There was also a room with padding on the floors, with balls and pillows and soundproofing. It was a place to jump and throw and yell, to let out your anger. I dipped my head into the doorway and grinned, thinking, *This looks fun.* A third room appeared like any daycare's playroom (dolls, trucks, blocks, and crayons), with one exception: the books on the shelf had startlingly direct grief-centric titles. Our tour guide explained how the little ones naturally transition among activities (move, play, sit.) She said that all of it represented kid grief, and that children knew how to grieve when you let them.

I hadn't been allowed to grieve. Anger tightened my stomach as I considered how easy it might have been for my family to give me what I needed. I fantasized for a split second about ducking into that padded room and losing it. Just as quickly, my body numbed. Instead, I tilted my head to skim the book titles while the group ambled back upstairs: *Losing Uncle Tim, Since My Brother Died, Why Did Grandma Die?, Someone I Love Died By Suicide, Am I Still a Sister?* While intellectually I respected the resources, I couldn't stop my torso from clenching with envy. Surely *some* books like this existed in 1992. Why hadn't anyone given me one?

When the next ten-week session started, the volunteer coordinator assigned me to facilitate a small group of eleven- and twelve-year-olds. Following our lesson guide, I started by inviting the kids to share their story of loss. Then, I simply listened without judgment. What I watched warmed my heart.

These weren't kids who were likely to hang in the same social circles if inhabiting the same middle school. One boy, for instance, wore fresh athletic wear and talked fervently about sports: a presumed future jock. Another favored heavy books and spoke with the vocabulary of a grad student. Yet these differences dissipated at the door. Each rediscovered their own voice as they eased into sharing, some diving into dramatic detail and others testing the waters by offering only generalities. In the way they leaned bravely into sharing something so tender, and in the way they listened to each other without wincing away, it was clear how they thirsted for this connection.

In the blink of an eye, this group of grieving adolescents went from feeling utterly alone in the world to befriending kids who were suffering just like them.

Years later, I read about this process in *Never the Same: Coming to Terms with the Death of a Parent* by Donna Schuurman. She writes that two foundational actions one can take to address a parent's death are to feel one's emotions and share them with others. The concepts sound so straightforward and simple when typed in a tidy black serif. Yet applying them in real life is anything but. In that small bedroom-turned-meeting-space that winter, I got to help a few kids through that messy process. Each week I sat amazed as their young hearts opened wider. It was thrilling.

One evening began joyfully when the boy with the advanced vocabulary brought in his sister's homemade chocolate-chip cookies to share. We gushed over how great they tasted: compliments to distract from the sorrow that filled the air around us. Their mom had died a few months prior after a multi-year battle with cancer.

He told us, "She won't stop baking. That's what she does when she's upset and doesn't want to think about it." My heart sank. We got quiet, our chewing and the occasional squeak of shifted chair legs the only sounds in the room.

I wondered if my brother, who was five and a half years older than me, had theories about my coping mechanisms. Although our family didn't speak about such things, maybe Aaron noticed how much time I spent alone in my room after our mom died, how quiet I became. He would have been just as tender as this boy, desperate for his sister to feel better but in the throes of grief himself.

As we transitioned into the planned exercises, I asked, "How does your loved one's death affect you at school?" That night, as with many others, I resisted the urge to participate in the activity I facilitated.

A girl answered, "My friends pretend like nothing happened." Her older brother had died in a car accident.

"Yeah," the future jock chimed in. He had lost his grandpa, who he and his five siblings had spent time with nearly every weekend. "It's like, they don't know what to say, so they just don't say anything."

Me too!

In everything those pre-teens shared, I saw myself. I knew it wasn't about me. I loved and respected the work of facilitating. I recognized that those kids had been catapulted into too much responsibility already, and it was their turn to have the floor. Yet part of me yearned to be heard. That part of me wanted to tell them about my third-grade field trip to Fontenelle Forest when someone said, *Mandy doesn't have a mom.* I stood frozen among the trees, angry but unable to speak, until one of the volunteering mothers came to my rescue. *Sure she does. Everyone has a mom. Some moms just aren't with us anymore.* Oh, how my little heart rejoiced at that rare acknowledgment of my mother's existence. Not knowing how else to cope, I held my story and emotions inside.

One night at the end of our two and a half months together, we created soft mementos to honor their loved ones' memories. I sat at the craft table helping the kids sew small pillows from their dad's old t-shirt, the quirky cat fabric their grandma would have liked, or their mom's favorite cotton summer dress. They'd carry it around in their backpack, take it out and hold it for comfort.

While an older volunteer helped run the single sewing machine, the kids and their surviving caregivers congregated nearby to await their turn. They were loud, laughing at family memories and swapping ideas for new memorial traditions.

I wished I had had something similar. All of my mother's clothes, including the unworn ones we'd gifted her the Christmas she was hospitalized, had been quickly hauled off to a women's shelter after her death. As a kid, I would have loved a pocket-sized pillow made from a fabric she'd worn. I would have loved to sit at a sewing machine—with anyone—and have the kind of conversations those families were having.

I remembered the previous year's project of working with a seamstress to convert my mom's wedding gown into a modern strapless one. Hers was handmade in daisy-edged polyester with long sleeves and a high neck, suitable for a Catholic wedding in the seventies. To fit my size six figure, the dressmaker loosened the seams as much as she could. She added a black satin waistband and layered extra daisies and sparkling beads over the bust. It was an impressive transition. It was also uncomfortable when I inhaled fully and didn't flatter my frame quite as much as I wanted for such a heavily-photographed day. Instead, I wore a stunning taffeta mermaid gown that I purchased off the rack after trying it on for my smiling, teary-eyed mother-in-law.

I had recently sold my mom's restyled dress on Craigslist to a random bride-to-be who was looking for *something cheap*. I didn't even take a photograph. My mom and then my dad had protected that garment in a cedar chest for over thirty years, yet within a year of acquiring it, I discarded it. Why did I have to be in such a rush to declutter? My stomach churned with regret while I helped the families clean up their mess of stray threads and fabric scraps.

The next morning, I woke up tired. It wasn't just the grief and jealousy that lingered, but the shame of them. I thought I was supposed to be over it by now.

Some things in life require direct, physical experience to reach true understanding, like music, making art, or making love. But is experience enough? All of my repeated exposure to grief had fooled me into believing I was a pro. Now, I felt like an absolute amateur. I wondered how I could have missed so much despite years of practice.

I enjoyed being with the kids, families, and staff at Mourning Hope. I had finally channeled the energy of my loss into something of value to others. Yet my first session as a volunteer facilitator was also my last. I expected to cry tears of empathy. I hadn't expected to snap open a bulging box of my own neglected needs demanding my attention.

I did what I thought I had to do, what I had done so many times before. I stuffed the swirl of emotions back inside the box where I believed it couldn't hurt me. I stayed away from the place that had riled them up. And I hardened my shell to keep them from breaking free.

1 NOW

I have thick skin.

"Just one last question," one of the men interviewing me announced.

In a few weeks, when I realize my devastating mistake, I'll recall the red flag of that final question. But that morning, seated at a shiny mahogany boardroom table and blasted by air conditioning that amplified my jitters, my focus was elsewhere.

My armpits swampy, I worried whether they could see the sweat through my blazer. I straightened my shoulders to bring my arms closer to my torso, then tucked my fingertips under my jeans to keep from fidgeting.

An hour earlier, Mark, the hiring manager, had greeted me in the software company's dim, echoing lobby. His polo and jeans confirmed that I'd nailed the wardrobe decision. I met his boss, Dan, a bit later when he bounded into the conference room in gym shorts and flip-flops, offering me a firm handshake as he announced his name and VP title. His confidence hit me like a physical force, knocking me against the high back of the office chair.

Eager to win this job with its twenty percent salary increase, I'd carefully prepared at home. I practiced behavioral stories about times I'd overcome challenges, felt proud of an achievement, and navigated an interpersonal conflict. I prepared smart questions to ask about the company's strategy and the problems they hoped the person hired would solve. It was the same level of disciplined preparation that had earned me a full college scholarship and *Exceeds Expectations* marks on performance reviews. And as usual, my self-control seemed to be paying off.

"Do you have thick skin?"

"I do," I replied with a smile, providing my most self-assured answer yet that morning. What they couldn't see about the petite woman sitting in front of them was that my skin was thicker than most. I didn't even cry at my mother's funeral.

Mark looked toward his boss, his expression reading, *Told you I found a good one*. But Dan wasn't so easily swayed.

"I don't know..." Dan started, shaking his head. "We're a different kinda place. You can't take things personally when you work here. Some people just can't handle it. You sure you're up for it?"

Was I sure? I was thrilled to be asked. "Absolutely."

Dan held eye contact, apparently expecting elaboration. I was happy to oblige, as I had recent proof to demonstrate this apparent prerequisite of employment. In personal and professional circles alike, I was often described as someone who *tells it like it is*. I was proud to be recognized for my honesty, and I expected the same kind of directness from my peers. Lately, though, my coworkers had seemed less open to my ways. In the last few months, I'd made two of them cry.

"The thing is," I began, "*I'm* the one who makes people cry where I work now." Pleasant surprise registered on Dan's face. "I don't mean to. It's just..."

My mind played back those heart-dropping moments when my teammates, each breaking from her typically strong persona, expressed how I'd made them feel. One peer wiped her wet cheeks while standing at my desk, asking why I'd rejected her repeated offers to help me write training materials. I was annoyed that she hadn't been more straightforward beforehand, when I'd assumed her offers were insincere niceties. A couple of weeks later, from the privacy of a small meeting room, our lead engineer shed tears while recalling how I'd challenged her in front of our team.

"It seems like people are so sensitive. Like, there was this engineer who said at our daily standup meeting that it was impossible to have work planned four weeks ahead of time. Which is bullshit, right?" They nodded in camaraderie over this near-universal challenge in the tech industry. "So I disagreed. Which is a totally acceptable, normal thing to do. But she made me meet with her in a conference room later and told me she felt 'disrespected.'" I raised my fingers in air quotes. "And, yeah, she cried."

I had been taken aback by her reaction. I was sorry for making her cry, but at the same time, I had been *right*. I couldn't understand why my accurate observations had upset her. She was a calm and capable professional, a leader on the team. And she cried over little stuff like that?

"So, believe me, I *love* that you're asking me about thick skin." I shook my head and crinkled my eyebrows, the recalled irritation tightening my features. "I'm tired of having to sugarcoat everything where I work now."

I worked at a place where I felt like I couldn't be myself, where I had to be careful not to step on more tenured toes, even when my ideas clearly led to productivity boosts. What a waste of energy. I didn't have time to soften my feedback in case someone wasn't willing to hear the truth. From my perspective, they were the ones with hurt feelings; they were the ones with problems to fix.

"I see," Dan said with a grin. "Alright then."

"You'll fit in great here," Mark added.

After we wrapped up, I strode outside to my sedan, squinting against the summer sun and reflecting on how well the morning had gone. I felt certain that an offer was forthcoming. From the driver's seat, I dialed my husband's cell. I kept the engine off despite the interior's thick humidity, anxious from the critical mental voice that warned, *Leaving the car running is bad for the environment! Are you that careless?*

"Hey!" Bob answered. "How'd it go?"

I appreciated his calm in big moments like this. He could do things I didn't have the patience-stamina for. Every winter he happily spent hours sitting motionless in a treestand to hunt whitetail deer. He could convince a cable company representative to reduce our rate without raising his voice or saying something he'd be ashamed to see in print.

"Amazing," I answered. "I think I'm gonna get the offer."

"Yeah?"

"Yeah. It didn't even feel like an interview. It was so easy, and they liked all my answers. Everything I've learned about the company and the team sounds like something I'd enjoy. But, yeah. It was good. Who knows, but I'm excited." I worried I was rambling and stopped myself.

"Good job, babe."

"Thanks!" I shrieked, grateful to have someone to share this joy with before going to work where I'd have to secret my enthusiasm. "I know it's not official yet, but *if* it happens... I'll make so much money!" It would be enough, I figured, for us to sell our suburban starter house and buy one of the condos we'd wanted the first time we went house-hunting.

"You earned it."

"I guess."

This was a back-and-forth dialogue so practiced that we could carry it out in our sleep. I would doubt my capabilities, then he would validate them, and I would discount his compliments. He was in love with me; why would I expect him to be impartial? Besides, no matter how hard I worked or how many goals I achieved, my mind seemed to generate an endless supply of evidence that I was still short of meeting expectations.

He ignored my deflection. "We should celebrate."

"I didn't get it yet!"

"We should celebrate the *interview*."

I hadn't thought of that, but maybe he was right. Maybe this was already enough of a success to enjoy. I wondered if it was arrogant of me to feel proud. "Okay, I gotta get to work."

"'kay. Love you, babe."

"Love you, too."

As I drove, the vent air cooling my skin, I thought about my potential future. The new company seemed like a perfect fit. For one, it was relaxed. I could hang up my business casual attire and sport jeans and t-shirts to work like so many of my friends did. I'd be able to cuss in meetings without being side-eyed. Plus, the role itself was one I'd been doing for two years already: I was good at writing requirements that solved customer problems and made sense to engineers. But what I was most excited about was what I'd learned in that final interview. If thick skin was a desirable trait, this might be precisely the kind of workplace where I could be myself. I wanted my bluntness, a core element of my authentic self-expression, to be valued instead of criticized as *too much*. I wanted to feel free.

What I didn't recognize that morning, before I made a simple career decision that would change more than I could have thought possible, was how wrong my self-evaluation had been.

Authentic self-expression was the opposite of what was happening.

Sitting in a rigid conference room chair beside my two new teammates, I opened my notebook to the next blank page, eager to learn.

At the beginning of my second week at the company, this recurring meeting appeared on my calendar with no agenda. I thought about asking one of my peers what to expect and if I should prepare anything. But sending an instant message felt like an unnecessary interruption, and I hadn't run into them in person.

Though we were eighty employees, I rarely saw more than a face or two at a time. Folks were hidden in offices and among rows of cubicles positioned for privacy.

Now that we were together, I asked, "What exactly is this meeting?"

"Just a team meeting."

Before I had a chance to ask a follow-up question, Mark and Dan came into the room. Soon, they were deep in a discussion across the table from us. I listened to try to establish the context, something I'd need in order to provide valuable input. Then I could secure my reputation as a Smart Team Member. I gathered that they were unsure how to test a new piece of software.

The conversation volleyed back and forth, Dan to Mark and back, circling a problem and seemingly getting nowhere. I wondered why my teammates weren't voicing their own ideas, as surely more diverse input would help. Their silence irritated me.

And then, I felt that excited fluttering in my belly that accompanied the thrill of solving problems: I had an idea. When a slight gap in conversation appeared, I took my chance.

"Maybe you could test it on a virtual machine." It seemed like a fantastic solution, though to be fair, I was only following about thirty percent of the conversation.

Dan snapped his head toward me, his round cheeks pink and his eyes wide with a sudden fury that awoke an ancient fear in my belly. In a menacing tone he spat, "Maybe you should focus on doing *your* job instead of worrying about his."

Shock traveled up my throat like vomit. As I fabricated a calm, complicit expression, I heard "okay" coming from my mouth. *What just happened?*

"We've, uh, already tried something like that," Mark added, shifting in his seat.

I nodded to him, as if his response resolved the ugliness that had just transpired, then looked down at my paper to take unnecessary notes.

The conversation continued like it began—without me—but I could no longer listen. I swallowed the lump in my throat between shallow breaths and blinked away tears before they had the chance to fully form. I cursed my flushed cheeks, an inheritance from my father whose rosy cheeks had earned him the nickname Apples. I focused all of my attention on maintaining my composure so that my emotional overreaction wouldn't be noticed. The last thing I wanted was to be judged as sensitive.

Concurrently, my brain scolded me for messing up. I must have done something wrong to cause Dan's anger. The thoughts were a melancholy song I'd heard repeated to the point of memorization. Of course it was me. I had done something terribly wrong before, hadn't I?

It was all so overwhelming that I wanted to crawl into a hole and disappear forever.

My teammates remained mostly silent throughout the meeting. I wondered what they were thinking. Had I been too smart, or too stupid? Too direct, or not direct enough? Could they tell why I was being quiet, or was I effectively camouflaging my internal chaos?

Maybe I needed to quit this job.

Once the meeting finally ended, I headed straight to my high-walled cubicle. I faced away from its opening, leaned over my notebook with a pen in my posed hand to appear busy to the occasional passersby, and replayed the meeting. It was embarrassing to be scolded in front of the whole team, but the way I was acting felt even more so. What the hell was wrong with me? I couldn't understand how one little comment could knock the wind out of me, could take me from having a perfectly fine day to barely holding myself together.

And holding myself together felt of utmost importance. I'd been packing away my feelings since grade school, when I spent my nights learning the language of step families and mutely missing my mom.

At lunch, I made the trip between cubicle and kitchen as brief as possible. I was afraid to run into Dan and feel my eyes moisten again against my will.

"Busy day?" A co-worker smiled at me as I brushed past her, balancing my steaming, recently-frozen lunch atop its cardboard packaging.

"Yep!" I replied over my shoulder, faking a smile. I hustled toward my cubicle, where my only distractions were an empty to-do list and dull employee manual.

The rest of the day dragged on like a gray Nebraska winter despite the sunshine outside. Motionless in my rolling chair, a cheap style that had shocked me in relation to the ergonomic one my last employer provided, I waited for the clock to strike five. I feared another annoyingly friendly face popping up out of nowhere to ask me why I was leaving early.

When I finally made it to my car and then out of the parking lot where someone might see me, I let out a big breath and felt tension release from my shoulders. I could have cried then, enveloped in the anonymity of the road, but the sensation had passed.

Later, pulling into our garage, I felt only a shadow of shame in my chest. As I stepped inside the house, our brindle boxer-coonhound, Keira, crossed the living room to greet me.

I loved my dog. She was playful, as soft as a teddy bear, and, unlike the stuffed animals I accumulated as a child, affectionate in return. I'd also always appreciated dogs' nonjudgment. With them, there was no performing. I could be enthusiastic. I could cry. I could even angrily kick her back hip when she stopped following my *heel* command. She'd still be right there with me, looking up with adoration. No excuses or apologies required. Relationships with non-human animals were so much easier than with humans.

Keira's nails clacked on the cherrywood floor as she approached. I patted her head briefly before heading toward the kitchen.

Bob greeted me as I entered. "Hey, babe!"

His cute crooked grin was like a shot of calm injected in my veins. Though what it meant to me had transformed over our eight years together, including three years of marriage, it was the same smile that caught my attention when we met on Freshman move-in day.

Back then, we had passed each other on the University of Nebraska–Lincoln sidewalk outside of the co-ed computer science dormitory where we would both live for four years. He wore a cutoff punk rock t-shirt, tanned biceps on display. He flashed me a friendly smile, slightly higher on the right, and introduced himself with an outstretched hand: *Howdy! I'm Bob.* His calm confidence surprised me even more than his offer to help me cart my boxy TV inside. I had been prepared to meet geeky, socially-awkward male classmates; I had not been prepared for someone so cool.

"Hey." I dropped my purse and keys onto our quartz kitchen counter. Then I busied myself with the nearby stack of junk mail, feigning interest in Express's latest pant sale.

"How was work?"

"Fine." *Oops. That came out more forcefully than I meant.*

"You okay?"

I looked up, my eyebrows bent with contempt. "What do you care?"

He straightened, apparently even more surprised than I was.

I wanted to apologize. I opened my mouth, trying to form those two simple words—*I'm sorry*—but the lump in my throat reappeared. I was sure something regrettable would happen if I made another sound: tears falling, a wail escaping, or some other sign of weakness.

I had to get out of there.

I closed my mouth and held our eye contact for a moment, hopeful that he'd pick up my telepathic message: *Stay here. I need to escape. Maybe I'll tell you about it later, when I'm not such a mess.* I hustled up the stairs and into our bedroom. I multitasked, kicking off my flats at the same time I closed the door behind me, tossing my earrings and wedding ring on the teak dresser while striding toward the bed. I glanced down at my clothes and thought, *Good enough.* In one graceful practiced movement, I pulled back the comforter and flat sheet, slipped my tired body into the bed, and swooshed the blankets back up over my head. My safe space.

I didn't notice Bob had come into the room until I felt the subtle weight of his hand on my shoulder. When I was grumpy, he rarely intruded. We were skilled at avoidance. But coming home and giving him the silent treatment out of nowhere was a bit next-level. I rolled over and lifted my head out from under the covers. He scooted onto the bed beside me.

"What's going on?"

I responded by not responding.

"Do you want to talk about it?"

No, but what are the odds that you'll leave me alone if I don't?

"It was just a hard day."

"What happened?"

I swallowed. My interview flashed to mind, Mark and Dan asking if I had *thick skin*. How could I have been so wrong about myself? I updated my mental chart, erasing that phrase from the *Me* column and scribbling it on the *Not Me* side instead.

We laid in silence for a long time, my body so numb it could have been unattached from my head, could have been a lump of matter belonging to someone else. I kept picturing my next team meeting, Dan's anger aimed at me. Finally, I murmured, "Maybe I shouldn't work there."

Bob responded in a voice that was even more gentle than his smooth everyday tone. "It's only been, what, two weeks, right? Shouldn't you give it a little more time?"

If he knew the ridiculous reaction I was having to something so trivial, would he have said the same thing? Or would he think I needed to hurry up and quit before someone realized what a baby I was?

After a moment he asked, "Have you been taking your pills?"

Three years before, I had visited a psychiatrist about my persistent blahs. She prescribed me an antidepressant after no more than twenty minutes of conversation. I was delighted to not have to share much of anything personal or painful, just the facts of my symptoms, losses, and family mental health history. I told her that my brother had been diagnosed with severe clinical depression as a young adult. I explained my dad's intense mood swings that neither my stepmom, Cheri, nor I ever understood. I told her about my mother's sudden death, and that she might have had depression, based on family rumors.

After I answered the psychiatrist's questions, she deduced that I'd most likely always had mild depression, contributing not only to the low days that drove me to her office but to high days that weren't as high as other people's.

I wasn't so sure. It seemed to me that I was fine as a little girl, before the world stopped making sense. And I hated the way she refused to commit. I *might* have mild depression, who knows, try the pill and see what happens. As if my life were some inconsequential experiment. But they had made me feel less shitty, less up and down, so I still swallowed one every morning after brushing my teeth. I just had to stop into her office once a year and smile, let her know that everything was hunky-dory, even when it wasn't so.

I sighed loudly, annoyed by Bob's question. "Yes, *Dad*, I'm taking my pills." As if I still needed a reminder.

"Sorry."

I rolled my eyes and almost imperceptibly shook my head, jaw clenched. I was just a total bitch, and that was all he had? Why couldn't he show some intensity for a change? I wanted him to yell at me like a normal human being.

My attention wholly focused on this newly-identified enemy, I snapped, "Would you just leave me alone?"

Bob stood and walked out of our bedroom, quietly turning off the light and closing the door behind him.

I gritted my teeth, irritated by his calm. Like a weighted cloak that tempered every upset, his nature contrasted the unbounded, erratic energy of my ups and downs. My reactions never made sense, which meant I couldn't figure out a way to control them. And I needed to be in control.

I lay on my side and commanded myself to cry now that there was no one to see me. But my eyes remained dry. I couldn't chill out all day at work, and now this? I was so frustrated I could have screamed. Instead, I threw the covers off and stormed downstairs to escape in front of the hypnotizing television.

My problem seemed immediate and isolated: an overreaction to a new situation. It didn't even occur to me that my drive to control my tears had been in place since elementary school.

2 THEN

I have to be strong.

I peered inside the casket, standing just inches taller than its side. My hands clasped together in front of my chest as if reciting the morning's *Our Father* with my second-grade classmates, but it wasn't God I spoke to.

I miss you, Mommy.

Covering my mother's entire scalp was the ivory polyester scarf my aunt and I had picked out at Kmart for the occasion. Pinned at her right shoulder, it was a style my conservative mom, fond of pastel turtlenecks and practical flats, would never have worn. But I knew it was because brain surgery had left her with a bald, stapled head. I pictured a pale peach scalp, the same shade as her face, and a smooth semicircle of tidy silver staples.

She didn't look quite right in her dress. Dad had told me that, since her brain was the only damaged part of her youthful body, we'd donated her other organs to save the lives of several terminally-ill people. I wondered if, to make her belly look normal, they stuffed her with wadded-up paper towels. I noticed that her boobs were a little too big and her waist a little too narrow.

Later, in one of the mortuary's side rooms where family lingered around a supersized submarine sandwich, my dad attempted to entertain the room (or perhaps distract himself) with endless chatter. He was the biggest and loudest member of our household. Heavyset since childhood, his upper-body strength had been maintained by years of lifting tires and engine parts as an automotive mechanic. I knew his might by the bear hugs that took my breath away and left me giggling.

That day, his characteristic enthusiastic storytelling, though out of place, lifted the energy of the room. Dad showed us the photo he had given to the funeral home staff: Mom at a party in a royal blue belted dress, her chest looking a size bigger than reality, her waist a bit smaller. Always armed with humor, he joked that she would've been pleased with the mortician's modification.

The funeral home was packed with people, including nearly every adult I knew and many others who I didn't. Even my second-grade teacher sat in the pews, and I couldn't understand why she had come to something that wasn't school-related.

At some point during the services, a woman I didn't recognize leaned down to speak to me.

"You've got to be strong now for your dad and brother," she said.

I do? I hadn't seen this as my responsibility, but since all adults seemed infallible at that age, I took her command to heart. I wouldn't cry. I didn't want to make my family sadder.

While the priest spoke, I sat in the front pew, secure between Dad and Aaron, whose shoulders towered high and comfortably boxed me in. I avoided their faces, staring instead at an imaginary spot on the carpet. If they were crying, I couldn't let myself see it. I wouldn't be able to hold in my grief a moment longer.

Later at the church, we once again sat in the front listening to the priest talk. This was our church, adjacent to the Catholic elementary school Aaron and I attended. It was the same school that Mom attended years before us, back when her mom was a teacher there. It had a high arched ceiling flanking a massive stained glass window of the Resurrection. I gaped at that array of colors during Mass twice a week, but I had never before been forced to sit so close. I squirmed when the priest stopped in front of me. Father Frank was my father's cousin and a man I loosely recognized from family reunions. I blushed when I realized he was talking about me to the crowd.

Before finally making his way back to the pulpit, he proclaimed with surety, "We can find comfort in knowing that LuAnne is in a better place."

I knew the place he referenced. Not long before, our yellow Labrador retriever was put down. When I told my mom I missed Cinnamon, she reminded me that the dog was in Heaven with Great-Grandma, God, and Jesus. I usually tried to follow directions, but picturing my mom in Heaven didn't feel good. Instead, my stomach tensed with anger. Wasn't *this* a good place, here with me?

The closed casket was wheeled to the aisle near where I sat. I watched the priest wave smoke over her and felt nauseated by my first taste of incense. I yearned for the smell to stop, and even more for them to open the lid *just one more time*. Then, I watched the casket bounce down the aisle on the backs of black-suited men.

Outside of the church, a shining onyx limo was parked at the curb.

"What's that doing here?"

"It's taking us to the cemetery," my aunt Mary Pat explained. "You wanna sit in the back with me?"

I was thrilled; I'd never been in a limo before. While hustling toward the open door of my impressive ride, I glanced across the lot toward the school's front entrance. There, a group of kids stood gawking at us.

"Hey!" one yelled out. "What are you guys doing?"

I wanted to shout at them *Shut up!* and *Stop staring!* Instead, I tucked my chin to my chest and scurried into the vehicle, out of the freezing mid-January air.

We drove to the cemetery where my mom was going to be buried next to my dad's mother, my grandma who had died of emphysema before I was born. The spot was partway down a hill between the quiet, curvy road and a cross-shaped cluster of hedges. When the formalities had ended, I followed my dad back up that hill, the frozen grass crunching under my shiny black dress shoes. I had made it through my mom's whole funeral without crying.

"Mandy!"

I turned to see who was calling my name and saw a woman who lived down the street from us speedwalking our way. She held a small floppy-eared plush dog I recognized.

My best friend and I once spent an entire day at her house after Mom encouraged it. Childless, she didn't have toys or games to entertain us. We searched her home together looking for ideas to pass the time. Before finding a pile of plastic bags filled with jewelry-making beads and string in a closet, I'd eyed a couple of tucked-away stuffed animals. Used to getting my way, I begged her to let me take that adorable puppy home, but she didn't cave.

Dad noticed her as well, and the three of us came to a stop just before the road.

"I... This is for you, dear."

For me?

"What do you say to the nice lady?" I got the sense that he didn't know who she was, which didn't surprise me. Between working two jobs, going out to golf or drink with friends, and tinkering alone in our garage, Dad wasn't around like Mom had been. It didn't bother me because I didn't know anything else. And because Mom had been my person.

"Thank you," I recited, grinning wide.

"You're very welcome."

She and my dad spoke for a moment, and then we continued our short walk back to the warm limo. I wasn't sure why I was getting a gift when it wasn't my birthday or Christmas, but I was glad. That fluffy big-eyed bundle in my arms provided a spark of warmth in my chest that outshined any thoughts of Heaven.

With the funeral behind us, the crowds of support simmered down. Much of our time was spent at home, just the three of us and the oppressive weight that had taken Mom's place.

One such day, we sat near the dry Christmas tree while Dad opened Mom's presents, the only remaining holiday packages. He took one from the top and tore off the reindeer paper: slippers. He looked at them for a moment, then put them on the floor, starting a pile.

The next box revealed a coral sweater. "I wasn't sure if she'd like this color." He half-laughed, "Guess it doesn't matter now."

My stomach hurt. Those were supposed to be my mother's gifts. Just a moment before, it seemed, she was there, leaning over my shoulder with a smile to earnestly examine the coloring page I held up with pride. Now, she was gone. Utterly, entirely gone. The strangeness of it was dizzying. But she *had* been there, I reminded myself, and that pile of gifts was evidence. That pink cable-knit sweater proved that she had been real. Unfortunately, Dad was destroying the evidence with each paper tear, each box she didn't get to see, each item she didn't get to be surprised by.

The world no longer made sense.

"This one's from me," Aaron said flatly, picking up a little box. "It's a bell. For her collection." He removed the paper slowly, revealing a cut-glass bell I found breathtaking. "We could keep it," he suggested.

"Yeah!" I yelped. "Can we?"

"Don't matter to me."

Aaron stood and took the key down from the top of the china cabinet. He opened its fragile glass doors, and then gingerly placed the bell between the others and a yellow ceramic chick I painted in preschool. Dad offered me a box to open, but for once, I shook my head.

When everything had been unwrapped, Dad and Aaron stuffed the crinkled paper into a trash bag and pushed the piles against the wall.

Ding-dong.

"More food," Aaron predicted.

Dad answered the door and came back holding a big silver pan.

"Here," he said, handing it to my brother. "See if you can fit this in the freezer. Otherwise, just leave it on the counter. We'll eat it tonight." Aaron went to the kitchen, Dad headed upstairs, and I went to my room. Solitude was now standard.

I suspect the generosity of so many individuals delivering homemade meals to our family was critically helpful. Dad wasn't the family cook, had three mouths to feed, and was newly grieving. It's a brilliant way for a loved one to lift a burden in an otherwise helpless situation. But the logistics of food prep passed over my little-girl brain. What I saw in those foreign casseroles was Not Mom.

I missed my mom's dinners, like pork roast with sauerkraut and my favorite potato dumplings. I missed her fresh-baked chocolate chip cookies, and how she, Aaron, and I would huddle around the counter licking sugary dough from the hand-mixer attachments, the spatula, or the emptied bowl. I even missed complaining about Brussels sprouts: turning away from Dad, who would insist that I eat them, and toward Mom, who would certainly budge once I'd complained enough. There was no more bouncing in my chair and gabbing about my day, raising my voice as Mom disappeared into the kitchen to refill Dad's water glass. I spoke, but it was less. It was tempered. It was uncertain.

That evening, the three of us sat around the dining table in our usual seats, careful not to glance up at the empty chair and the stark space now available on the vinyl tablecloth. We ate orange goo from a deep disposable foil tray. Dad assured me that it was macaroni and cheese, but it wasn't anything like the blue-boxed mac and cheese I knew and loved.

"Why's it taste like that?" I said, my nose crunched.

"Cuz this is *real* cheese," Dad said. "It's not from a box."

"I don't like it."

"You ought to be grateful. Kids are starving in Biafra."

I didn't know what Biafra was, though it brought to mind the frightening images of emaciated African children I had seen on weepy television ads. From my perspective, that was hardly relevant. I was the one who had to eat the weird mushy noodles.

When we finished, Dad carried the leftovers to the kitchen. I followed Aaron, picking up a dirty plate. Aaron stopped in the doorway and turned around, smirking. He crinkled his nose, stuck out his tongue, and pointed an index finger toward his throat.

I giggled.

"What's so funny?" Dad asked.

"Nothing!" we responded in unison.

When Dad said it was bedtime, I went alone to my room. I tried not to remember the way Mom used to lean against my headboard and read to me before tucking me in with a kiss and a song.

Once the holiday decor was packed away, we rarely talked about Mom or what happened to her. Everyone else seemed to prefer it that way.

"That little girl hardly ever says a word."

I sat cross-legged on my sitter's living room carpet half-watching music videos. My ear was tipped toward the kitchen where Cathy spoke on the phone in a hushed voice. If I had been a few years older, I might have been too transfixed by the shadows playing on Jesus Jones's face to have noticed that she was talking about me.

Cathy, a heavyset older woman who walked with a cane, lived across the street from us. Widely considered our nosiest neighbor, my dad and his friends privately nicknamed her Chatty

Cathy. After Mom died, Dad recruited her to babysit me for an hour or so on school days.

Though she was using the voice she always used when she didn't want me to hear her phone conversations, I had heard enough to know that I was the current subject. It was true that I had become quieter since Mom died.

"I bet she won't tell anyone when she gets her first period."

My cheeks burned at the mention of menstruation. At eight years old, no one had yet uttered my name and *period* in the same sentence, unless they were praising my grammar. I felt embarrassed and, more than that, misunderstood. She was wrong. I had faith that by the time the distant future of puberty rolled around, I'd have someone to tell.

Her conversation continued more clearly as the song on the television ended. "I don't think anyone's brushed her hair since it happened. It's a rat's nest on that girl's head."

My stomach dropped. Did I look funny? Was *everyone* talking about me the way Cathy was?

As soon as I saw Dad's truck through the front window, I slipped on my coat, shouted my goodbye, and ran out the door, hustling home. Once inside, I dug around under the bathroom sink, my best guess at where Mom might have kept my hairbrush. My job had been to sit still while she styled, not to retrieve her tools. Gratefully, I found it. I added *brush hair* to the overwhelmingly long mental list of tasks for which I was now responsible.

I carried the purple brush around the corner to my room, glancing past Aaron's open door on the way. Seeing his disheveled waterbed made my stomach feel hollowed out. He was gone, like usual.

An independent and grief-stricken thirteen-year-old with friends old enough to drive, he was increasingly not at home. I missed barging into his room and acting silly to make his best friend laugh, kicking my feet to Technotronic from my perch on his waterbed, or having him show me again the braided lanyards he made at 4-H camp. I missed playing Nintendo on his television set: *Duck Hunt* with plastic guns and the cute dog who whimpered and barked, or *Track & Field* with the big mat that he complained I jumped on too hard.

Now, on the rare occasions when it was just the two of us, I wondered if he thought about Mom as much as I did. But I didn't ask. I couldn't. My throat closed up before the question had a chance to become sounds.

Once inside my bedroom, I stood in front of the dresser and took in my reflection. My appearance wasn't something I often judged. Usually when I stood in that spot, I practiced arranging my brunette strands into the exciting styles Melissa Joan Hart wore in *Clarissa Explains It All*. I didn't have her wide headbands, frilly barrettes, or bright scrunchies, but I made do with an assortment of simple ponytail holders. I never braved leaving the house with my unique ponies and braids, afraid of being teased. Instead, I'd ask Mom to execute one of the two or three bland but certifiably acceptable styles I'd always worn. It had been two months since I'd had her help.

I sat on the edge of my bed and tugged at my tangles. In time, I would learn how to hold my thick, wavy hair near the scalp when brushing so that loosening the knots wasn't so uncomfortable. But that day, the bristles of the paddle brush kept getting stuck, causing sharp bursts of pain. I brushed until my eyes were filled with tears.

I stood, placed the brush on my dresser, and suddenly caught a whiff of cleaner. That winter, after Mom died, Dad hired a woman to clean our house every other week. With a huff, I stomped twice to my left and flung open my closet door. Just as I had suspected: my shoes were lined up on the floor. They didn't belong on the floor. Mom kept them in the top left dresser drawer, next to the atrocious red rubber device she sometimes used to suck snot from my nose. Every time this woman came, she moved them. I had complained to Dad, but nothing changed.

I crouched down and began to move each pair back to the drawer where they belonged, grunting in frustration. When I finished, Dad appeared at my door.

"You hungry?"

"Nuh-uh."

As he turned to leave, I called after him. "She did it again!"

He stopped. "Huh?"

"My shoes! She keeps moving them!"

He grinned. "Be ready to go in thirty minutes." As he walked away, I wondered how he could be so indifferent about a near stranger defying my mom's rules. But I quickly forgot about my frustration. I was excited because tonight was the night I was going to meet his girlfriend, Cheri, and her two-year-old daughter, Melissa.

My dad started dating Cheri about a month after my mother died. They knew of each other from high school but hadn't cared to see each other after graduation. Our backyard neighbors, Louie and Linda, were friends with both my parents and Cheri, who was recently separated from her husband. Linda encouraged their first date. Since then, my father left home often to see Cheri. I looked forward to having a mom in the house to dote on me and cook the homemade dinners I considered normal. I was especially thrilled to meet Melissa. My best friend had a little sister, and I thought it would be so cool to always have someone to play with.

I stretched out my pink and white striped blanket on the carpet beside my bed and arranged my many stuffed animals in a rectangle around its edges. My friends, as I thought of them, included Henry, the Union Pacific railroad conductor dog, and two Glo Worms. I had a yellow Funshine Care Bear and a cheerleader with my name, Mandy, written on the chest of her shirt. My favorites were the four Cabbage Patch Kids dolls including a blonde I renamed Stephanie after the Full House character and a brunette Crimp 'n Curl, coincidentally named Melissa, that Mom had bought me that Christmas. The newest was the gray and brown dog our neighbor had gifted me at her funeral.

I sat on an edge and stroked the soft blanket a few times before going on. "Okay, everybody," I announced in a burly voice, bobbing the white bear whose belly read *Playtime Bear*, "It's playtime." I continued in my own voice, "Thanks, Playtime Bear!" Then I read to them from my favorite book, *Go, Dog. Go!*

Before I made it to the canine party at the end, Dad shouted from the hallway. "You guys ready?" Aaron must have quietly arrived home while I was playing.

Dad popped his head in my door. "What are you doing? We gotta leave. Get your shoes on!" He left as quickly as he'd appeared.

I couldn't simply stop reading and leave, I thought. Henry was a very sensitive dog whose feelings would be hurt.

"*It's okay, Henry,*" I whispered in my tiniest voice. "*Don't cry. Do you want your hat?*" I smoothed the floppy miniature conductor hat onto the plush brown head. "*There. I'll be back soon. Promise. Playtime Bear will take care of you while I'm gone, won't you?*" I hugged the toy to my chest, set it back down in a seated position, and hustled to meet up with Dad and Aaron.

The three of us put on our coats and walked around the block to the neutral territory of Louie and Linda's house. Linda led introductions in the crowded kitchen just inside their door. Then Aaron followed their teenaged son into his bedroom while the rest of us gathered in the living room.

I sat beside Dad on the sectional. Across from us, Cheri sat upright on the other couch with Melissa on the floor. An adorable toddler with big brown eyes framed by long lashes, she bashfully hid her face behind her mom's legs and grinned whenever someone tried to pull her into the conversation.

Though I had been excited to meet Melissa, I was grateful for her shyness. It took some of the adults' attention off of me, and I was struggling to interpret what was expected of me. This was a new type of adult-child relationship in my world. How do you act around a dad's girlfriend? Was she more like a parent's friend to whom I was supposed to speak seldomly? Or more like an aunt with whom I could talk heartily about myself? It was safest to keep my mouth shut. So, the adults soon gave up on trying to engage me in their conversation and chatted while I observed.

When I learned that my dad had a girlfriend, I pictured someone thin, blonde, and large-chested like the women on TV he tended to comment about. I was surprised that Cheri was normal looking: a short, strong-jawed brunette with a perm. Instead of the confident and outgoing personality I expected, she spoke infrequently and politely while my dad carried on like usual. I was blind to the stress she must have felt meeting her widowed partner's children. The situation dampened her personality. Taking in the conversation as if it told me everything I needed to know about this woman, I couldn't understand what made her special enough for him to choose her so often over us.

My confusion swelled to resentment. What gave her the right to take up so much space in his life when I was already down one parent? I certainly didn't ask. I was getting good at holding in my unwelcome feelings. I was strong.

3 NOW

I need a new job.

Slouching in my swivel chair on a quiet afternoon, I glanced to my right to make sure no one was passing by before opening a new browser window. The wing of the building in which I sat was darker than I preferred. An engineering manager who sat nearby had unscrewed half of the fluorescent bulbs in the ceiling because he didn't like their harsh brightness. When I asked him about opening the blinds for natural light, he didn't want that either, citing the heat.

Most days in this job, I was bored. Being new to both the company and the financial industry we served, I had traded in my status as Subject Matter Expert for Least Valuable Player. There were minimal onboarding resources, and because my teammates were swamped with deadline-driven work, they pressed forward without me. Therefore, the few tasks Mark had assigned to me were either brainless or well beyond my knowledge level.

But it wasn't just the boredom that troubled me. Where some people center their lives on their religion or family, I had always focused on my career. At my youngest, I wanted to be an artist. With age and schooling, the ideas became more practical: a radio DJ because I loved listening to music, an EEG technician so I could help people with brain aneurysms, a CEO because my eighth-grade English teacher suggested I was qualified. There were always ideas and action plans.

This pursuit satisfied more than an innate interest in the working world. At home, I didn't hear the words of affirmation I craved. But at school, my intellectual achievements never went unnoticed. Teachers adored my curiosity. And if they weren't vocal, a piece of folded paper at the end of the quarter served as a suitable substitute. I was good at learning and following the rules. I could recall every mark that didn't meet my expectations: the ACT score that, even after three tries, was two points lower than that of a classmate I wanted to beat; the B minus in undergraduate physics; and the differential equations class I withdrew from to avoid a poor grade during an overbooked semester. Since college, the only time I could recall disappointing an employer was when I resigned.

With my shift into a company and role where I wasn't adding value, I felt completely out of my element. To cope, I often distracted myself.

That afternoon, I was having one of my high-energy days, a time when I powered through projects with focus, be they actual work or personal. I had finished what tasks I could and, desperate for something at least mildly fun, planned to shop from the convenience of my cubicle.

I clicked through a few pages of Amazon results, scrolling past bulky upholstered bar stools. Our new home had a bar-height kitchen island that could double as a dining table given the right set of stools. I was on a mission to find something minimalistic but cheap.

My higher-paying job gave Bob and I the opportunity to sell our house in Lincoln and buy a newly-remodeled condo in Omaha. We both enjoyed the walkable downtown entertainment district in Omaha, the state's biggest city, and the move cut my work commute in half.

I grew up in Omaha. When I left my dad and Cheri's house at eighteen, I landed in Lincoln an hour away for college. I moved further away to St. Louis after graduation. A few years later, I returned to Lincoln: circling my hometown but not entering. Now I had finally returned, but not to my suburban teenaged stomping grounds. I had, in a sense, returned to my birthplace.

The house my mom and dad had owned on Vinton Street was only four miles from our new condo. I saw the green rectangular *Vinton* sign every time I headed down Thirteenth Street toward the interstate that cuts east to west through the city. When I drove to the grocery store, I passed by the library I had been inside so many times with my mom.

That's my old library, I'd report from the passenger seat of Bob's Subaru each time we drove by. The Willa Cather branch is a brick mid-century modern building with a roof angled to the sky and a front that's all windows. One glance and I would be transported to unrushed days spent roaming its aisles, lined with shelves twice my height. I would grin, remembering the time Mom let me check out a VHS that read *Belly Dancing* down its brown plastic spine. I was disappointed when later, from our den's couch, I realized that the boring hip shaking was never going to advance to what I had imagined belly dancing to be: rotating on the floor on pushed-out bellies like spinning tops.

I copied links to my two favorite barstool sets and pasted them into a chat to Bob. He was busy, but I couldn't wait for him to *not* be busy. I spent large swaths of time alone in my cubicle running down the clock, while he hurried from meeting to meeting, or from state to state, for his work. That day he was driving across Nebraska to meet with a client. I figured he could make time to help me decide about the chairs when he got to his hotel room after dinner. Plus, I could rely on him to not complain about it.

My task complete, I looked away from the monitor for a moment and noticed that I really had to pee. I pressed the keyboard shortcut to lock my screen and headed that way. As I turned into the central hallway that housed the restrooms, I heard

Dan's voice getting louder and felt a rush of adrenaline, my bodily systems on red alert.

Dan hadn't again shocked me quite as much as in our first team meeting exchange, but he remained inconsistent, vacillating among friendly, dismissive, or harsh. Though I didn't have to interact with him much, I saw him in the halls most days and was on guard each time he was near.

I rushed to the women's room door, escaping inside before Dan made it into my line of sight.

By the time I returned to my desk, confrontation successfully avoided, my heart rate had slowed to normal. Having completed my bar stool research, I opened the job description I'd recently bookmarked: community college IT instructor. It was a part-time gig I thought I could do in addition to my full-time job, the kind of role that might eventually grow into a second career. I glanced to my side again, decided to reduce the browser window to about a third of its height, then clicked the *Apply Now* button.

My days weren't always this fruitful. Some days I was quiet and unproductive, and would crawl into bed after work, unable to speak. Others, I'd spend the day tense and come home raging to Bob about my boss's incompetence. I had never failed. So, what was happening now, I needed to see as someone else's fault. I blamed all of my frustration on Mark, who apparently expected me to learn through osmosis the complex accounting regulations that our software automated. Against my intentions, my negativity sometimes spilled out among my coworkers, who reacted by giving me wide berths.

Energetic, deflated, touchy, detached: I never knew what mood would come next or when the shift would occur. It was as if little live wires had spread through my body, their wild ends shooting sparks of electricity that threatened to collide and set off some kind of never-before-seen explosion.

I tried to run from them. I told Bob every handful of days that this was it, I was going to quit without notice, never speak to any of my coworkers again, and spend my days alone and in bed.

I tried to calm them to stillness. I made lunch plans with the few friends who I trusted might have something useful to say about the depression I was battling despite consistently taking my prescribed antidepressants.

In my more optimistic moods, I tried to connect them into one aligned energizing wire, propelling me toward meaning. I filled out all of the best *ideal career* assessments I could find online. I copied the summarized results these webpages delivered, lists of my *fields of fascination* and *core life purposes*, and emailed them to Bob. I brainstormed business ideas. Health coach? Business consultant? Personal organizer? Custom gift crafter?

It was one such mood that had led me to the job opening I was now re-reading. I filled in the names and dates of my previous employers and thought back on the moment in grad school that made me believe I wanted to be a professor.

I had been shopping on a mild summer afternoon in St. Louis's upscale Central West End district when I saw my Ethics professor lounging at a cafe table. He looked like freedom personified with a newspaper in his hand, one jeaned leg crossed loosely over the other, and a coffee cup nearby. I embellished the image over time so it had become a movie, lively and uplifting. His friend appears—she'd been running late, rushing from her corporate gig, a black business suit her uniform. He smiles up at her warmly, his delight a sharp contrast to her flustered arrival. I wanted to be him, not her. I wanted that self-assuredness, that laissez-faire attitude. I wanted his peacefulness.

I copied the application questions into a blank Word document so I could spell-check my answers. I let the fantasy consume me because the present seemed unbearable. My body had been overtaken by uninvited feelings that I couldn't control. I felt stuck in the eye of a tornado, powerless.

I didn't want to be stagnant, but moving didn't feel safe, either.

I lifted my vibrating cell phone from the long island that separated the kitchen from the open living area and read a text message from a friend.

miss your face. we should hang out soon! next weekend?

My heart sank. I didn't have the energy to reply cheerfully. I certainly wouldn't be able to go out with her. I looked up to find Keira sitting tall and motionless beside her elevated bed, staring at me as if to plead for a walk. *Not tonight,* I told her with my eyes, the self-disappointment multiplying. I noted the time (just after seven) and slipped my phone into the butt pocket of my skinny jeans.

I missed my evenings: trying out a new recipe, devouring self-help books on the couch, or working on craft projects. But after who-knows-how-many nights crawling into bed early, hardly able to speak let alone organize an evening of leisure, I was exhausted. I thought that taking the day off from work would help. But here it was, evening already, and I was still so tired. All I wanted was my bed.

As I nudged open the door of our spare bedroom, the soft evening light angled into the space. The only glow in the room came from the laptop screen. Bob was lounging in the office chair, legs resting on top of the desk, ankles crossed. Opposite his slippered feet stood a tall can of Pabst Blue Ribbon. Bob had gotten used to me quietly crawling into bed shortly after dinner, and I'd found that he wouldn't ask questions as long as I kissed him goodnight. He reached toward the keyboard to pause a video, then swung his legs down and sat up tall.

"I'm going to bed," I said. "Good night." I leaned in for a quick kiss, impatient for the warmth and solitude of bed.

He reached forward, wrapped his arms around my waist, and put a hand on my ass. As I tried to pull away, he leaned in closer and kissed my neck, slow and wet. I crunched my face in disgust. It was clear that he wanted to make love. Meanwhile, sex was the last thing I wanted. Bob did this all the time, as if someday he'd find me in a state of profound arousal while I was doing the dishes or getting dressed in the morning.

It wasn't just that I didn't want to have sex that night. I was fed up with the expectation that I would reject my own wishes in order to satisfy someone else's. But I knew no other way. My bones held the memory of being told at my mom's funeral to *be strong* for my dad and brother, an implication that the emotions of the men I loved were my responsibility. They held the stories of my mom bending herself into a mold she hoped would please my dad: rushing back to the salon when he didn't like her new perm, roasting him duck late at night when he came home hangry from the bar, and taking him back after he apologized for losing his temper.

My world was full of protocols I couldn't stand adhering to but that, when broken, triggered shame. And I was breaking them more and more. Over the past few months, as the depression drained my energy, my ability to put on a happy face and follow the rules had become seriously inhibited. It was as if a resentful, ignored part of me wanted so badly to rebel that she was shutting down the operating system in a desperate last-ditch effort to get my attention. I wouldn't say Yes to him tonight, but I didn't feel good about it. *Poor Bob*, I thought. I *wanted* to want to make love.

"You're sexy," Bob whispered in my ear.

When our faces pulled apart, my expression had turned to guilt.

"You okay?"

I was surprised when what came out of my mouth next was a shout. Anger pulsed through my torso and found its way out of my mouth before I could trap it. "You always want to have sex!"

A pause. "It's been nine days." Was he seriously keeping track?

"Then why don't you jack off?" It was that simple, wasn't it? I stormed out of the office, back through the kitchen, and down the hall toward our bedroom.

Once in my pitch-black room, I started to slam the door shut. The strength behind that initial pull felt so satisfying. Then, I remembered the loud bang that was sure to erupt when the door met its frame. Into the future I imagined Bob's frustrated face and heard his scolding, disappointed words. I caught myself mid-swing and slowed the movement of the door as much as possible in its final arc. I cringed when it slammed anyway.

I tossed my phone on the window sill, slipped off my jeans and bra, then crawled into bed without brushing my teeth.

I hadn't meant to shout at him, but it was so hard to interact normally when I felt anything but. I wished I didn't feel so irritable all the time. I was especially clueless about how to handle the anger. I resisted it in myself, wanted to leap past it. Lying there on my side in bed, it felt like my shoulders were up to my ears. I flipped onto my other side.

I didn't understand why my reactions were so extreme. I had never felt like crying at my previous job. But part of me knew that even while workplace situations were triggering much of my stress, my job wasn't the root cause. I'd experienced similar sadness before. I went through a rough patch just after college, one during college, and even as a kid. I'd been experiencing sadness bigger than the people around me since nearly as far back as I could remember, since Mom died.

As soon as the memory landed, I rejected the idea that her death was relevant. I recalled how, in high school, I even wrote an essay about the tragedy and my comforting conviction that *Everything happens for a reason.* I didn't pause to wonder what I had meant by that thesis. I didn't notice that I hadn't communed with that faithful version of myself in quite some time. Instead, an image I'd seen on the National Geographic channel entered my mind: steady, straight-backed women carrying big baskets of produce atop their heads. Didn't they ever slouch against their heavy loads?

I noticed I was holding my breath and inhaled. I flipped sides again. Eventually, I fell into a restless sleep.

When I woke up, my right forearm was cold. It was outstretched, silencing the alarm on my cell phone. I rolled over and closed my eyes.

"You gonna go to work, babe?"

Surprised to see Bob was already showered and dressed, I wondered how many times I'd hit *Snooze*. I really didn't want to get up. I shrugged a half-covered shoulder.

He turned away, slightly shaking his head, and returned to the bathroom.

I couldn't go to work in my state. I couldn't even speak to answer Bob's question. My feelings were stuck in me like gum in hair. I grabbed my phone from the nearby ledge and opened the email app. *I'm still not feeling well*, I typed with my thumbs. *I need to take another sick day*. Surely two unplanned sick days were less conspicuous than showing up depressed after one? I hit *Send*, and my shoulders relaxed. I'd done everything I had to do for the day.

I put the phone back and rolled over, sweeping the bedspread up over my head. I turned my face toward a little fold in the blanket that created a space for breath. I rested, legs curled under me like a fetus, squeezing an extra pillow in my arms.

I heard Bob approaching and felt annoyed by the loud smooch of him kissing my cheek through the blanket. "Love you."

I listened to him take Keira out, bring her back inside, and lock the front door behind him.

My belly was tense. I cried into a pillow, letting the sobs come out loud.

My nose was stuffy. I thought I should grab the roll of toilet paper before it started running, but my body felt so heavy. I wiped my nose with the sleeve of my sweatshirt instead. The tears kept coming.

When I felt a massive stream of snot rush out of my nose, I finally dragged myself out from under the covers. I speedwalked into our bathroom, head tilted all the way back, eyes on the ceiling behind me, to keep the mucus from running into my mouth.

Back in bed, I drifted in and out of sleep.

Later, I lay wide awake, listening to the sounds of traffic, of people walking down the sidewalk, of my stomach growling. I got up and lowered the blackout blinds a touch to let in a sliver of daylight so I wouldn't have to turn on the actual light to make my way back into bed.

I stood at the kitchen counter, my hands hovering in the small cloud of warmth above the toaster. My heart sped up as I imagined nosy neighbors peering in at my disheveled hair, puffy red eyes, and tear-stained cheeks. Keeping my face turned away from the windows, I rushed back to bed with my plated snack.

I sat halfway up in the semi-darkness, leaning against the headboard and pillows, and slowly chewed bites of buttered Italian toast. It had long been my favorite snack, but I couldn't taste it. Mom used to make me cinnamon toast with a mix of sugar and cinnamon sprinkled heavily on top. Thinking of her, I felt lonely. Would she have understood what I was going through? Would she have been able to help?

My brother once told me our mom had been depressed. Aaron and I had become penpals. I was a junior in high school, and he was imprisoned across the country on drug-related charges. Since it wasn't something I'd observed firsthand, I asked if he'd ever talked to her about her mental health. He hadn't. He wrote, *I read her diary once, but that's about it. No one in the family was real talkative about that type shit.*

That my mother had kept a diary was an exciting revelation. I was desperate to get my hands on it. Unfortunately, Aaron assured me in a subsequent letter that it was *long gone.*

When I asked around as an adult, my relatives disagreed about her emotional state but agreed that she hadn't, to their knowledge, kept a diary. I hated that answer. Wouldn't a diary be an unavoidable discovery when going through a dead person's possessions? Maybe it was mistaken for a notebook of household to-dos and trashed. Maybe Dad did know about it and, for her privacy or his own, got rid of it before anyone could read it. Or maybe Aaron was mistaken. Maybe what he had found was a one-time journal entry, scribbled in a sad moment in an attempt to sort through scattered thoughts. This is what I chose to believe, that it had never existed, so I wouldn't feel its loss so acutely.

I had trouble imagining how she'd respond to my present situation. Besides, they were pointless questions, I thought, since I was on my own now.

When I noticed my plate was empty, I put it on the floor and re-entered my cocoon.

I opened my eyes to the sound of a key in the front door. If I had considered Bob's need for affection, I might have stood. I might have walked to the entryway and given him the hug he'd once told me made him feel loved after a day apart. Instead, the realization that it must be after five weighed me down with disappointment. I had hoped the feelings would have gone away by then.

Soon, Bob flipped on the bedroom light and joined me in bed. I lay stiff on my side with my eyes squeezed closed against the irritating brightness. He curled behind me.

"I'm taking my pills," I asserted, a defense against a nonexistent offense. *I don't know why, since they're obviously not helping.* I wondered how many refills I had left. I'd be too far from fine to fake a cheerful check-in with the shrink this time around.

"I'm worried about you."

He was worried about me? The words shook away some of the fog that had been clouding my mind for... well, I wasn't sure how long. Bob rarely expressed concern over my wellbeing, and when he did, he tended to be right. He talked me into getting a checkup so I'd have a primary care physician, should I ever get sick. He encouraged aloe vera cooling gel on a throbbing sunburn. In college, he pushed me to end the silent treatment I'd been angrily giving my best friend for weeks.

Upon hearing his words, my brain dutifully shifted into analysis and problem-solving mode. It thrust itself above the grime that had formed a dusty film over my day-to-day in order to consider potential cleansers.

On the one hand, Bob remained the only person who knew that I moped around the house and spent so much of my free time in bed. That was a good thing. I didn't love the idea of making him worry, but it was a contained risk, wasn't it?

On the other hand, when the sadness came on, it was impossible to hide it at work, so I'd been taking a lot of sick days. I didn't want to risk losing it in front of my coworkers. Any day now, my boss could confront me about my lack of observable physical illness symptoms. The image terrified me: Mark awaiting a justification with an accusatory stare, arms crossed across his chest, and the other guys at work standing behind him as reinforcement. What would I say? What *could* I say?

If I wanted to keep my job and my pride, something would have to change. But I couldn't see an acceptable path forward. Therapy was the most reasonable next step, but I dreaded the idea of laying out the authentic mess of myself for another human to scrutinize. With counseling, I saw two potential outcomes. One: They'd be revolted by the real me, by the culturally unacceptable thoughts and feelings I meticulously hid. That would confirm my fear that I was different from everyone else, broken in some profound way, and would never belong. Two: They'd be bored by the real me. They'd announce that everything swirling inside of me was unimpressive and my own damn fault, and I needed to just get over it. The problem was, I'd already tried that method and failed. If they didn't find anything diagnosably wrong, it meant that I'd be like this forever.

"Maybe you could talk to someone," Bob offered as if reading my mind.

I shrugged.

"We have insurance. Plus you can use the fake money." His tongue-in-cheek nickname for our health savings account didn't elicit my usual grin. He probably thought the only voice in my head discouraging counseling was the penny pincher. I wasn't going to correct him, my fears too paralyzing to verbalize. Like Beetlejuice, it seemed that speaking them would make them more real. So instead, I put up my armor.

"They can't do anything anyway."

"What about the lady you saw in St. Louis?"

He was referring to a therapist I saw briefly in my early twenties when the transition from college student to employee took its toll. I had been relatively honest with her, and she hadn't judged me. She labeled my lingering dead-mom grief as normal. Ultimately, she helped me reconnect with two of the three people who first loved me.

Bob had a point. This evidence countered both of my feared outcomes. Plus, there was something so attractive about learning precisely what was wrong with me. If the right professional spent enough time studying my situation, maybe they'd be able to diagnose me like they did my brother. They'd give me a treatment plan; they'd deem me fixable. Sitting with a stranger and admitting to my shameful reality would be tough, but it just might work. My chest faintly tingled with possibility.

Some ideas have to be nudged into our awareness many times before we'll listen.

I opened my eyes. This was a path forward that I was willing to take. I rolled over to face Bob, my body lightened by a breeze of hope, and sighed out a breath I hadn't realized I'd been holding.

"Maybe you're right."

He kissed my forehead.

Though I could see the path ahead of me, I couldn't yet clearly see the path I'd already walked. I didn't understand that this moment was merely a reincarnation of the cyclone that had come before. Though my workplace worries were new, this was the same swirl of fear, resentment, and hopelessness that I had felt in the disorienting years after my mother died and changes abounded.

4 THEN

I'd rather be dead.

Nine months after meeting Cheri, I stood alone near the new artificial Christmas tree in our front room and craned my neck to see what was happening beyond the picture window. Aaron and Dad had just gone out into the cold, and though I couldn't see the driveway from where I stood, I realized that Cheri must have arrived.

As far back as Easter, Cheri and Melissa had been tagging along to our family get-togethers. Now, they were around more often than any of the relatives or friends with whom we used to spend time.

The differences I discovered between my dad's girlfriend and my mother disappointed me. I expected her to be gentle and doting. Instead, she encouraged us to be tough, covering her daughter's cuts with kissless bandages. She wasn't into any of the pastimes my mom had enjoyed, like tending her vegetable gardens, refinishing antique dressers in our garage, or walking down the street to chat with elderly neighbors. Instead, Cheri liked to talk on the phone with her mom, sister, and friends. She shopped for clothes. My frugal mom spent the weekends in my dad's old race car t-shirts and gray sweatpants cut into shorts. Cheri would never do that. She wore color-coordinated outfits. I stopped visiting the Willa Cather branch of the Omaha Public Library and got to know the Gretna Outlet Mall.

Cheri also didn't cook like my mother. Even when foods were familiar, they weren't the same. For instance, my mom would let Aaron and me nibble on the red rubber coating from bologna slices. Then, she'd add the cold cuts to sweet mayo-lathered bread. Cheri instead threw the whole slice into a skillet, fried it, and served it with tangy mustard. When I questioned her strange choice to heat the meat, she looked at me with a puzzled smirk. *Because it's a* fried *bologna sandwich!* she'd said, as if I was the weird one.

I don't remember if Cheri asked me what condiments I preferred with my bologna. But even if she had, I wouldn't have answered. It hurt to recall what I had lost. And whether it was for my comfort or my caretakers', the unspoken rule had been ingrained: don't talk about Mom. The avoidance was modeled by every adult around me. How could I possibly describe those sandwiches without acknowledging the woman who prepared them?

I heard car doors opening and closing, then felt the burst of cold air when the front door opened. Dad walked inside toting a black plastic lawn bag in each hand. He walked upstairs without remark. Cheri followed closely behind in much the same way, wearing her bulky winter coat and carrying a paper shopping bag on each wrist. Aaron came next with a third lawn bag, smirking at me before heading upstairs himself. It was the same smirk he flashed when we teamed up to tease Melissa.

Melissa was with her dad that night. Her parents had separated just before we met. Most of what I knew about divorce came from Rainbows, a school program that Dad and Cheri made me attend that year after the teachers' urgings. Unlike me, every other student in the small grief support group was coping with their parents' divorce. We filled out workbooks that had questions like, *How do you feel when you're at your other parent's house?* I would sit in silence with teeth clenched, angrier with each share. I knew I was supposed to feel sorry for them and believe that we had something in common, but I didn't. What did they know about loss? From my perspective, there could be no greater contrast between us.

I glanced down at the empty space under the tree and wondered what I'd get. Usually, presents from Mom and Dad would have been piled high by then, a few days short of the holiday. On Christmas morning, after setting out cookies the night before, a few fun unwrapped gifts from Santa would appear. I would have written out a numbered wishlist weeks before, each item labeled with the ad and page number where I found it, if applicable. I would have handed it to Mom while enthusiastically explaining each item. That year, no one had asked me to write down my list.

I looked back up at the window. Every December, Mom and I decorated that window with red, white, and green decals. She'd let me arrange the wintery scenes and help me place the letters in the correct order to spell out *MERRY CHRISTMAS* or *HO HO HO*. Then, we'd step back and admire our festive display. Now the large window stood bare, nothing to see but the tall bushes that paralleled the walkway and the charcoal sky beyond. Cheri had seen my mom's stickers in their storage box and declared them tacky. I touched my finger to the cold glass and imagined feeling the slick surface of a leaping vinyl reindeer.

Behind me, I heard the group reemerging from the stairway. "What are you guys doing?"

"Stay there," Dad commanded. "No coming upstairs, you got it?"

I stood confused while I watched the three of them travel back and forth again between the driveway and upstairs. Eventually Aaron stepped out of line and wandered over to me, a look of ornery glee curling his lips upward.

"What are you doing?" I asked again.

"What do you *think* we're doing?"

I shrugged. "What's all that stuff?"

"Presents."

"For me?"

"You, me, and Melissa."

My stomach leapt in excitement. The volume contained in their many bags far exceeded what was typically under our Christmas tree.

"From Santa," he continued with a vicious smile.

That year, more of my classmates were saying that Santa was made-up. And while I didn't want to believe Aaron, it had been awhile since he'd deceived me.

A while back, his favorite trick involved a pair of silver toy handcuffs. He challenged me to break free, promising to release me if I couldn't, but then delayed my liberation until our mom or dad noticed. Once I'd learned how to wiggle my wrists free, he upped the ante. The last time he cuffed me, it was to the tree in the center of our front yard. He wedged his skateboard between the trunk and my hands so I had no slack to free myself. He left me alone for what felt like hours, and though I quickly forgave him, I also finally stopped letting him snap those cuffs on me.

He quit playing tricks on me after Mom died. For the most part, he was instead polite and subdued. The playfulness between us was gone.

I didn't yet know how to navigate this confusing world I had been thrust into a year before, but I knew one thing for sure: Aaron was experiencing something strange and painful, just like me. My heart felt nourishingly intertwined with his, bonded by the tethers of our shared tragedy. At the same time, a wall had erected between us that blocked the ease we used to enjoy in each other's company.

"Santa's not real," he continued.

I kept staring at him, hesitant to accept what he was sharing but recognizing its likely truthfulness all the same.

"They're the ones that buy us that stuff," he continued, pointing behind his left shoulder, "and they just *say* it's from

Santa. Come on, kid, did you really think some fat guy came down the chimney?"

"No," I lied, wondering how I could have believed in something so magical.

Later, when the job of shuffling around bags had finished, I repeated Aaron's announcement to Cheri to further test its validity.

"Aaron said Santa's not real."

"Well, yeah."

I stared at her, my voice caught in my throat.

"Oh, come on, you didn't still believe in Santa did you? You're nearly nine years old."

Did I respond? Did I defend myself with an assertive *No* or stand silent and dumbfounded? I don't know. What I remember is the familiar chain reaction of emotions. My feelings were hurt, but that was too tender a place to be with no one to soothe me. Next came the denigrating voice in my head who chided me for causing my present pain by failing to predict and then control the situation. This triggered a churning shame in my gut. Then, my body went numb, a reaction I was perfecting.

At the end of third grade, our house on Vinton Street sold. I didn't know what it meant to move, other than that it was going to require me to change schools. I didn't want to leave the classmates I'd known since kindergarten. I secretly liked a cute brunette boy in my class who paid me no attention. I could no longer watch him play basketball with his friends and daydream about him secretly liking me, too. Only Mom had known about my crush. Now no one did.

After we'd packed all of our belongings, Dad invited me to say goodbye to my lifelong home.

First, I stood in my room looking at the empty closet. Just inside the door to the left was where I would hide the gifts I made for Mom. I remembered the beaded necklace I crafted her for

Mother's Day, or maybe her birthday, and had forgotten about for a long time. When I rediscovered it and gave it to her, she didn't mind that it was late; she liked it.

"Dad, you forgot the curtains!" I exclaimed when I noticed the sheer rose fabric still adorning the windows of my former bedroom.

"We don't need 'em," he answered.

From the tiny hallway outside of Aaron's and my bedrooms, I said a mental goodbye to the bathroom. I used to trace the wallpaper flowers with my finger while I sat on that toilet. In that bathtub Mom had taught me how to spell turquoise: T-U-R-Q-U-O-I-S-E. I was sure I was the only one in my whole third grade class who knew how to spell that word.

I peeked into Aaron's room, but it held much less meaning without the waterbed, sports pendants, and our dead dog Cinnamon's red collar hanging from its peg inside the door. Besides, Aaron and all of his things were coming with us.

He was almost fifteen by then. He often left the house with giggling girls who stopped by the house to see him. When just the two of us were home, we watched TV together in the den, like the new MTV animated series *Beavis and Butt-Head*. We still avoided talking about Mom.

Just beyond the hallway was a door that led upstairs to *the brown room*, a big combination storage and playroom, wood-paneled and carpeted in brown shag. I spent hours there, sitting in front of the six-room Barbie house that Mom and Dad had built for me. I admired its carpet made of fabric scraps, staircase with a tiny twisted handrail, and real working lights. Occasionally Aaron was bored enough to command a dramatic battle between his G.I. Joes and my well-dressed dolls. There wouldn't be room at Cheri's house, and everyone said I was getting too old to play with Barbies, so we had gifted the toy to one of my younger cousins.

As I said goodbye to our house that day, I sped past the steps like usual. Beyond the brown room was my parents' room, which now terrified me. I had developed the fearful belief that my mom was a ghost living in her former bedroom. I had seen plenty of spirit-centric *Unsolved Mysteries* by that age. Whenever I passed, I monitored for signs of Mom-turned-evil-specter: a gusty draft, a flickering light, an unidentified sound. If I wasn't careful, I thought she'd float down that dark stairwell faster than I could blink, and she'd get me. What did *get me* mean? Why had I become an enemy? I didn't ask myself those questions. The fear of knowing always stopped me before I imagined more of the scene.

When it was near time to go, I returned to our hallway and stared up at the gold sconce that jutted out of the wall well above my eye level. I felt an urgency to memorize its appearance. The sensation was similar to what I had felt a year and a half before when holding Mom's dry hand in the hospital, willing myself to remember its texture. Back then, I hadn't understood exactly what I was losing. Now, at nine years old, given that both my mom and her father had died, I knew more about permanence. I was sure I'd never step foot in that house again.

And that house held my whole history of Mom.

That summer, the five of us squeezed into Cheri's two-bedroom ranch house while our parents searched the suburbs of Omaha for a bigger, newer home. I shared a bedroom with Melissa, and Aaron slept on a pull-out couch in the basement.

One evening late that summer, I lay awake in the top bunk, the comforter thrown over my head and tucked in all around me. I held my Glo Worm and squeezed his belly so his face illuminated my tiny tent.

When Dad had asked me to downsize my stuffed animal collection for the move, I had a hard time deciding which of my two Glo Worms to keep. In the end, I imagined that the older green one, father to the newer blue one, bravely volunteered to be the one to leave home.

Don't cry, Glowy honey. I wiped my finger across his plastic cheek, and then across my own. *I know you miss your daddy. I miss him, too. But he's in a better place now. He's with a littler kid who needs him more than we do.*

I wanted to cry loudly like I imagined Glowy was doing because I missed Mom so much it hurt, but I couldn't with Melissa sleeping right below me. If she woke up, she'd tell Dad and Cheri, and then I'd have to make up a story about why I was crying: a stomach ache, maybe. The only pains I'd seen either of our parents acknowledge without judgment were physical ones.

It seemed unfair. Melissa got to have her mom, and she still cried all the time. She bawled when I hid her beloved green Baby Bop dinosaur doll, and when I held the knob of her bedroom door in place to convince her that she was locked in. *You know, your mom could die, too,* I imagined telling her. *So stop being such a baby. There are more important things to cry about.* I got in trouble with Cheri every time I said something mean to Melissa, though, so I didn't go that far.

Under the covers, I wished I could be alone, and at the same time, I didn't want to be alone. I wanted it to be like it was before. If I could just talk to Mom once more, I thought, everything would be a little better. I longed to travel back in time. I'd have to keep my time traveling a secret, since knowing about her upcoming death would make her feel awful. Plus I imagined you could mess things up if you changed history too much. But even one minute talking with her would be magical. Or maybe a day, or a year? I figured I could go a full year without telling her she was going to die soon. I would do anything to see her again, to hear the voice I could no longer fully remember, to smell her perfume so I could memorize its aroma, to have a conversation.

Most importantly, I wanted a chance to apologize for all of the ways I'd hurt her.

The Christmas before the terrible one, she'd bought me the Susie Scribbles doll I'd begged for after seeing it advertised on TV. But when I saw its drawing capabilities, more true to its name than the masterpieces I'd expected, I felt betrayed. *I don't want this stupid doll*, I'd stomped. Eventually, Mom took it back to the store, instead gifting me with a new Cabbage Patch Kid and a few more doll outfits. But she couldn't take back her drooping face.

Once, when she was reading me a bedtime story, I pouted and put my hands over my ears as if I couldn't stand her voice. I wanted to say I was sorry for hurting her feelings, and that I loved when she read aloud to me.

I was especially sorry for my behavior the night before she went to the hospital. I remembered what my dad had said while I sat beside him on the den couch not long after she died. *I heard a noise that night when she came to bed*, he'd said, his gaze toward the wall across from us. I had perked up, desperate to learn more. I wanted to know why she got sick and went to the hospital. I wanted to know why she died. *She must've fallen, maybe hit her head on that nightstand*, he continued. *It was real loud like that.* Was that how she started bleeding inside her brain? *Must've been so tired from getting the presents ready for you kids*, Dad continued. *Then she got into bed. Didn't say a word.*

I didn't know that he was describing signs of a ruptured brain aneurysm, rather than the steps leading up to one. I didn't understand that he was likely processing his own guilt. What I heard was that she died because she hit her head, and she hit her head because of my presents. And that same night, I had whined and refused to help her with chores. That's what made her tired, wasn't it? That's what made her fall, and hit her head on the nightstand, and...

Unable to change the past, I looked to the future and wished for death. I squeezed my eyes shut and put my hands together under the blanket so I could pray what had become my usual prayer:

God, please let me die.

I knew from religion class that if I killed myself, I'd go to Hell, so I hoped God would find another way. Still, I had considered potential methods. Guns were too scary. I didn't trust my aiming ability. I feared that, instead of shooting right between my eyes and dying, I might blow off part of my face and have to live that way. I once saw someone on TV to whom that had happened. I considered cutting my wrist but expected the blade would hurt terribly. Instead, when enraged, I'd push my right thumbnail into the biggest blue vein on my left wrist, willing it to bleed. It never did. I thought perhaps I could stop myself from breathing by holding my face in a pillow. It seemed both the least painful and least risky approach. Every time I tried, though, my whole body would begin to shake. Soon after, I would be powerless to prevent my next breath. What I needed for it to work was someone to help. Someone *just* dumb enough. I closed my eyes, grinning.

I had the perfect plan.

The next morning, Melissa and I were in her room debating what game to play next. I walked to the window on the back wall and peered through the aluminum slats to make sure our parents were still in the backyard.

"I have an idea!" I announced with a big, fake smile. "Let's play *sit on the pillow*!"

"What's that?"

"See this pillow? I'll lay here on my back." I moved down to the carpet. "I'll put the pillow on my face, like this—see? And then you sit on top of it. The game is, you have to stay sitting. I'm gonna try to get up, but no matter what I do or say, you *have* to stay on the pillow, okay?"

"But I'll hurt you."

"No you won't, I promise. It's fine. Just sit right here when I say, and don't get up, no matter what."

I rested my head back on the carpet and put the pillow on my face. "Now."

Surprisingly, Melissa followed my direction, centering her little butt on the pillow. I grinned with hope and held my breath. Soon, she was helping me hold it longer than I ever had. *This might work!* I thought with excitement. My throat throbbed, urging my lips to part. My legs shook. Seconds later, a deep, cooling breath filled my lungs and sent a shiver of relief through my limbs.

Then my brain caught up to what had happened.

"Why did you get up?" I yelled, frustration coursing through my veins. "I told you not to!"

"You couldn't breathe."

"Oh my god, Melissa, you're such an idiot. If you can't do this, I'm not playing any more." I stared at her, hoping she would want to try again.

She looked back at me.

"Fine," I said. "Then get out of here."

"But it's my room."

I hated that tiny house, the way we lived on top of each other and I was never alone. "I don't care. I'm older than you, so you have to get out when I say."

"You said you wanted to play?"

"Yeah, well... you're the one who can't stay sitting on the pillow, which is, like, the easiest game in the whole world."

While Melissa stood looking at me, my mind flitted through past sibling experiences. Aaron had always been able to bully and manipulate me. I had to put up with him burping and farting in my face, relentlessly calling me a quitter for leaving my boring tee-ball team so I could play Barbies, and once peeing into my bathtub water. From what I could tell, he hardly got in any trouble for how he treated me. Now, it was my turn. I deserved to be the bossy one and get away with being a bit cruel when adults weren't around. But I couldn't get Melissa to do what I said. The injustice made me furious.

I squeezed my face and leaned forward before speaking slowly. "I hate you."

Her lips turned down and her big brown eyes glistened. "I'm telling my mom!"

A lead weight dropped to the bottom of my stomach as I realized my mistake.

"No, don't! I'm sorry. I didn't mean it, okay?"

She turned, opened the door, and ran down the hall toward the back door yelling for her mother.

"Please don't tell!"

Great, I thought. *Now Melissa's crying, and Cheri's gonna give me another talk about how I need to* watch my language.

I swallowed the lump in my throat while rummaging through the stack of toys in the corner of the room for a book. I dropped onto the floor cross-legged, book opened to the middle to pretend I'd been reading, and thought through my lie. *I didn't say I* hate *you, I said I* ate *you. I* fake *you? I* take *you? Yeah, I was saying I* take *you... to ride your bike out front! She just heard me wrong.*

"Mandy!" Cheri called out from her tiny kitchen.

Stupid book, you aren't even helping. My stomach churned as I imagined the book giving me the same sad face Melissa had. I gave its cover an infinitesimally small pat. *I'm sorry, Mister Book, you're not stupid.*

When I walked into the hall, Melissa was finishing telling her side of the story. I stopped in the kitchen doorway, eyebrows raised in mock nonchalance. "Yeah?"

After a year and a half, Cheri had become family. Sometimes it was fantastic, sometimes it sucked, and sometimes it was both in the same moment. Earlier that summer, for instance, she'd arrived home with new clothes for me. When I argued, Cheri pointed out the bulge of my stomach. I wasn't ready to let go of the clothes my mom had ordered from her thick JCPenney catalogs, and I was crushed to think of myself as fat for the first time. Yet the white sandals she asked me to try on, strappy with metallic seashells on the toes, were awfully cute.

I never dropped the *step* from her moniker. You only get one mom, I'd thought as a child, so to grant Cheri the title would be to erase my first. I did, however, adopt the term *parents* when referring to her and my dad. It was a sensible shorthand that did no more than acknowledge their relationship, I rationalized.

Regardless of what I called her, I loved Cheri. I may not have always liked her, but she was my sole surrogate mother figure. At a less conscious level, I yearned for her affection. Maybe that's why I spent so much energy judging her.

This, however, was not a moment to win her over. I was in crisis avoidance. I had messed up and wanted to get away with the lightest sentence possible. The only challenge was that I was still flush with frustration.

"What's going on here?"

"What?"

"Don't play dumb with me. You see she's crying."

"So what, she's always crying."

"Sit."

I slid the chair closest to me out from the table and plopped down.

Cheri asked again, "What's going on?"

Like I'm gonna tell you. She wouldn't like what I'd said to her daughter, so it seemed best to avoid the particulars.

"Why would you say something like that?"

"I didn't say anything!"

I realized with relief that Melissa hadn't shared about the pillow game. Close call. I had no clue what I would have said if questioned about that. Staring at Cheri and trying not to see Melissa's tear-streaked cheeks in my peripheral vision, I vowed to never again involve her in my death schemes.

"I don't *ever* want to hear that you've said something like that to her, you understand me?"

"Whatever," I huffed with an attitude more typical of hormonal teens.

"Amanda Lea!"

"What? I said 'whatever', like: yeah, okay."

Cheri shook her head and looked out the screen door into the yard. Dad was bent over in the sun, fiddling with the lawn mower. She looked back toward me. "Go sit on the couch and think about what you've done to your sister. And don't move until your dad or I come in and say so. Got it?"

I nodded, glad for the confrontation to be over, and hustled around the corner to the front room. I sat on the scratchy couch and started to put my feet up until I remembered that wasn't allowed in this house. *Don't put your dirty feet on the furniture*, Cheri had said. I heard them both walk outside, the screen door whacking closed behind them. The house was quiet again.

I was frustrated that my plan hadn't worked, and frustrated to be in trouble yet again for a situation that, if instigated by Aaron, would have never resulted in a timeout. Life wasn't fair.

Later, when I was getting so bored I thought I might risk standing up in rebellion, everyone wandered back inside and invited me to join them in the kitchen for sandwiches. My behavior was never spoken about again.

There was so much that was never spoken about.

By then, I had started acting like my usual self: hyper and talkative more often than quiet and withdrawn. When teachers scolded me at school, it was for giggling with my deskmate or passing notes. To my extended family, I seemed to have fully rebounded. I was *resilient*, they told each other with pride. I didn't feel resilient. I felt broken, split into two selves: the animated girl people saw and the one who silently cried after dark.

My suicidal ideations continued into middle school, when I wrote a brief will on a scrap of paper that I hid in my closet. Whether I followed through or died of other means (a freak accident, I imagined: something as sudden and meaningless as my mother's ending), I wasn't going to let Cheri decide who got what, the same way she got to decide everything. My toys would go to Melissa, a few CDs would go to friends, and the rest of my possessions, including a small amount of saved cash, would go to Aaron.

No one asked about my grief. I don't think anyone in my family ever suspected that I had suicidal urges. My brother was the only possible exception. Once, he found my doodles of a bullet speeding across the lined page from handgun to anonymous male profile. *What's this about?* he'd asked, thrusting the open notebook under my nose. *Nothing.* I don't think I could have been open if I'd wanted to be. I didn't understand why I had a compulsion to recreate that drawing. It was just a way I had found to express the thoughts of death and violence that raged inside me. He pestered me a bit more, and when I offered no detail, he suggested I never draw something so sinister again, lest it give someone the wrong idea about me.

I stopped drawing murder scenes. And somewhere before the end of high school, the suicidal urges quieted, drifting away as slyly as they had appeared. But my two selves remained.

5 NOW

I'm broken.

"Come on back," Mary said, inviting me into her office again.

The month before, inspired by Bob's nudge and the memories of what therapy had done for me in the past, I had searched my health insurance provider's website for a therapist. I chose Mary because she met all of the criteria I knew to consider: in-network, female, and located close to my workplace.

An older woman with feathered auburn hair and a gentle demeanor, Mary stepped aside so I could walk through the unpainted wooden door. Her office was packed with furniture that was in vogue twenty years prior: a large oak desk, a floral loveseat, two plush armchairs. I judged her taste and assumed she read up on modern psych research as infrequently as she adopted interior decor trends.

Now, I sat in the same chair I had for my previous sessions and wondered what unspoken analysis my seat selection prompted. If necessary, I could defend my choice with sound logic. It was near but not too near the armchair I'd accurately assumed she'd select in response. Plus, it was within arm's reach of a bowl of foil-covered chocolates. But did always selecting the same spot signal an undesirable personality trait? If I had sat on the far end of the couch, would I have seemed more relaxed and open to change? What if I had gone so far as to lay on the couch, a position so exposed I could hardly imagine doing it? Surely that would have seemed pathetic.

Our appointments usually progressed similarly. Outside of her office, I hadn't felt the urge to cry all month. But when settled into her chair, after sharing about work or how I had been feeling, tears would flow.

That day, after exchanging pleasantries, I didn't share anything before the tears came. They dribbled down my cheeks ceaselessly, like a leaky faucet in a dive bar bathroom sink. My other self had shown up and wasn't going to relent. I didn't have an explanation for my behavior, and Mary accepted my wordlessness. I was embarrassed to be paying her to watch me cry. More than babyish, it seemed irresponsible, as it made rational self-analysis all but impossible. But I couldn't stop myself.

I worried about the sessions' usefulness. Five years earlier, Bob and I had seen a relationship counselor for pre-engagement guidance. We weren't having issues. We just thought it would be prudent to pursue something like the premarital sessions of our married Christian friends before making a lifelong commitment. She had an easy, friendly smile. Visibly relieved by what our lack of conflict meant to her day, she tended to direct us toward lighthearted topics like wedding planning. The one valuable takeaway was her introducing us to Gary Chapman's *The 5 Love Languages*. I learned that I need words of affirmation, while Bob most appreciates physical touch. But we weren't guided through the comprehensive conversations our friends had spoken of: financial philosophies, desires around having children, whether we'd use spanking to discipline said children, and many other topics I couldn't recall but worried were of utmost importance. Ultimately, even though I had begun with clear expectations, they weren't met.

Now, with Mary, I was far less clear about what I wanted. I didn't have any friends who had resolved depression with a therapist and then given me the play-by-play of their sessions. I had no unbiased third party who I felt comfortable asking and no relevant firsthand experience beyond the few grief-focused sessions I had in my early twenties. How could I expect to get results if I didn't even know what to ask for? How would I know whether my expectations were met if I didn't have any?

When she broke the silence, it was to say, "You must really be hurting, Mandy."

Her nurturing words landed as warmth in my chest, but I was too afraid to accept them. In less time than it takes to blink, I revolted, scooped them out, and careened them from my awareness. *No shit, Sherlock*, I thought, channeling one of my stepmom's sarcastic catchphrases. Mary had a bad habit of interjecting meaningless statements between my sobs. What was the point?

"Yup," I replied with force, resisting an eye roll, then reached into the bowl on the squat side table and extracted a chocolate.

In Mary's reticence I chose to see incompetence: a fawn staring blankly at approaching headlights. And I was determined for her to remain as such until she proved otherwise. Meanwhile, I would be judicious in how much I lowered my armor.

I let the candy melt in my mouth while I folded the foil under my fingers. If the tears were here, so be it; that didn't mean I had to expose the thoughts that accompanied them. As the downpour slowed, I blew my nose with tissues from one of three boxes placed around the office.

When our time was up and I had confirmed my next appointment, I noticed that breath-giving sense of relief that had only recently become familiar. After this appointment, as with our others, I'd be able to get through my work days without needing to contort my face into a faux-chill expression. It was a peace I hadn't felt in months. I didn't trust her yet, but I couldn't argue with the results. I'd keep showing up until she gave me a reason not to.

Despite my fervent resistance, I suspect part of me knew that what Mary offered was precisely what I needed. It was not at all what I wanted, so I didn't see it. I could only see a well-paid underperforming service provider, gaudy furniture, and, worse, my own shameful lack of self-control. I couldn't let that continue for long. To lose control of myself was dangerous, which wasn't a conscious thought so much as a visceral sensation: something my body remembered.

My step-grandpa, Dawn, lay crunched up in a hospice bed in the middle of his living room. In a hopeless attempt at comfort, my family had piled at least a dozen pillows around him: under his head, under his bent knees, behind a bony shoulder.

Nine months earlier, he was diagnosed with pancreatic cancer, the same disease that had taken his dad and my mom's mom. By midsummer about six months later, he had lost so much weight that sitting still for more than a few minutes was unbearable. No amount of couch cushion could make up for the lack of butt fat.

Now, while I was in therapy and feeling increasingly well, his health was quickly and dramatically declining. His fingers, neck, stomach, and legs bloated with retained fluids. The cords of his portable oxygen machine dug into puffy cheeks. His legs were naked because of a high fever. Cheri and her sister, Denise, took a turn heaving his body onto its side enough to change his diaper and run a cool sponge along his sweating back. Their brother and my dad hovered nearby awaiting their shift. I stood back with Bob in the adjacent dining room and watched with wide, anxious eyes, glad to play a less active supporting role.

My stepfamily and I were both close and not close at all. As a kid, I had spent nearly every Sunday with them, hanging out with cousins and eating massive Italian dinners in the carpeted kitchen of Cheri's childhood home. After high school, my participation waned until it was only on major holidays that I showed up. With Grandpa Dawn's deterioration, I wanted to be more present.

Grandpa was a strong-willed and independent man. Years before, during a friendly family debate about life support, he had said, *If I can't take care of myself, just take me out into a field and shoot me. I don't want to die like that!* Now, he lay limp with his neck bent at an unnatural angle, as he'd slipped lower from where he'd been positioned. My dad leaned over Grandpa's right side, wrapped muscled arms around his chest, and nudged his body, some hundred-and-fifty pounds of deadweight, higher in the bed. "Poor Mike," he wheezed.

When the movement in the room had stilled, I sat next to his bed in a wooden chair I'd carried over from the dining table. I was going to try out that technique where you think about people who have it worse than you, so you can make yourself feel better about your own situation: starving kids in third-world countries, being burned alive. With faux optimism, I started, "It could be worse!" I didn't know what I was going to say next, but it didn't matter. The appalled look in his eyes stopped me. "Sorry," I said, cringing at myself.

That night at home, I went online and read about the final stages of terminal cancer. *What is it like for Grandpa right now?* I wondered. *How can I be helpful?* Curious why he hadn't died yet, I read that some people preferred to pass alone. Their family would slip out of the room, and they'd perish quickly. Or sometimes they'd think their family wasn't ready, so they'd hang on and wait for permission to pass.

The next day at work, sitting in front of my monitor but entirely distracted, Cheri called. Grandpa had been moved into a hospice facility. Before this rapid decline in his health, I had been preparing for an upcoming work trip to Buffalo, New York. Now I suspected that Grandpa could pass any day, and I wanted to be with my family. As soon as my decision was made, I went to Mark's office to let him know that I wouldn't be traveling.

Empathetic, Mark shared a story more personal than the ones we typically exchanged. He had once decided to travel for work, he explained, even though his mother was sick. She passed unexpectedly while he was away. He supported my decision: he didn't want me to experience the regret he carried.

Dan wandered in then, and I repeated my decision. His reaction was disbelief.

"Come on, no bullshit. Is your grandpa really sick?"

My jaw went slack. "Yeah," I snapped. "He is."

"Oh. Okay. I'm... I'm sorry to hear that."

I was flabbergasted that he had questioned my integrity. It made more sense later, though, when I learned that he had noticed me leaving several afternoons. Unaware of my mental health issues, he thought I was interviewing for other jobs. He was wrong about my dishonesty, I assured myself. I'd never heard back about that part-time college instructor job, and even if I had, it wasn't exactly a replacement.

Over the next couple of days, I took some time off to be with my stepfamily at the hospice center. One afternoon, while the other women in the family were taking a break, I sat alone in a hard-backed chair by Grandpa in his small, sterile room. I gently toweled off the clear liquid that had started to ooze from the top of his right hand. This simple act of helping in such a helpless situation, a role I hadn't been able to play in earlier deaths, provided a satisfying burst of self-assurance.

With his restless kicking, the blanket had fallen to one side, revealing a pale leg and the white edge of a diaper. It occurred to me then how artificially we live our day-to-day lives, wincing away from others' bareness when to lean in is not only harmless but essential. Leaning in cultivated the kind of loving human connection that science had shown us we'd literally die without. I remained beside him ready to provide whatever I could to reduce both his and my discomfort. Mine wasn't a burning cancerous pain but rather a desperate longing for his face to relax, for his lips to smile again.

"You don't need to be here," he breathed. "You've done more than enough already."

I bent forward, unafraid of the shadowy Grim Reaper waiting nearby. "I want to be here. I love you."

Those words carried more truth than most things I'd said lately. They stood in stark contrast to my striding through the office with faux self-assuredness amid a leader who deflated me, and responding to my counselor with a highly-edited subset of my embarrassing beliefs. They were nothing like walking on eggshells around Dad and Cheri, pretending along with them that we were unaltered watching our powerful patriarch disintegrate before our tired eyes.

As the days passed, he lost the ability to speak, and I remembered my research. I started to question how much time I spent in his room. Was I causing him more suffering because he wanted to pass in privacy?

Sitting beside Grandpa, the two of us the only ones in the room, I held his right hand. I spoke loudly now so he could hear, given his deteriorating senses. "Okay, Grandpa. I'm going to leave you alone now. Do you want to be left alone?"

He looked at me, lifting his head from the pillow and opening his eyes wide, as if pleading for me to stay.

"Okay," I replied, feeling certain for the first time in days. "I'll stay."

He relaxed his head back down onto the pillow. I relaxed into the chair.

After less than a week in hospice, he was gone.

Several evenings later, in the wake of Grandpa's death, I sprawled out on our couch and urged my tears to flow. They refused to follow my commands. Bob joined me, squeezing in close so we both fit.

"Grandma said something interesting," I started.

"Yeah?"

"Yeah. I was kind of afraid she wasn't dealing with it, ya know?"

"Mhm."

We hadn't seen her cry and, prior to the very end, I hadn't heard her talk directly about the change we all knew was coming.

"She said she and Grandpa weren't able to talk much about it because every time they did,"—finally, my tears began to fall, and I caught my breath—"they'd both start crying."

Bob grew teary too. "Even knowing what it would be like, he still did it."

"What do you mean?"

"The chemo and everything… He went through all of that so he could live as long as possible." A few beats of silence passed before he finished. "I want to take better care of my health. Enjoy life more."

We were touched by my grandpa's death in different ways. Bob was moved by his will to survive and saw a productive path forward for himself. Craving more intimacy, I was moved by their long-lasting love. Watching his final decline shook me out of my habitual thought patterns, bringing what mattered into focus: loving others, accepting myself, telling the truth.

But it didn't last. I didn't know how to turn my dreams of easy, authentic relationships into my reality. Those intense moments shared with my family only served to highlight the distance that remained between us after the immediacy of caretaking had passed. I could no more easily speak honestly with them about my feelings after than I could before.

Growing up, it had always been my brother with whom I confided. Though we tended to avoid the most difficult subject, our mom, we talked about everything else. He accepted me. But I soon lost him, too. And when he chose to leave, I worried that I'd misjudged his love for me.

6 THEN

I need my brother.

Knock, knock.

Eleven years old and upset by an overheard conversation, I stood outside my brother's bedroom door with my jaw clenched. I was eager to vent to the one person in our household who understood me.

"Come in."

I turned the brass knob and pushed. When I saw him smile the tiniest bit at the recognition that it was me who'd been knocking, rather than Dad or Cheri, my face muscles relaxed.

Aaron's role shifted after our mother died. Gradually, unable to handle everything myself, I softened my shell for him. Although I maintained my two halves, sadness tucked safely away in hiding, I regularly revealed my bitterness and frustrations. He, in turn, fell into the role of my surrogate everything. In fourth grade, I wrote a short story about the experience of our mom's death titled *Just the Two of Us*. The *us* didn't refer to my mom and I but to my brother and I. Though he escaped with his friends whenever they were available, he provided me with an invaluable safety net when he was present. I had lost my mom, but I hadn't lost the need to be mothered.

I closed his door behind me and sucked thick air into my nostrils, pulling in the scent of his Drakkar Noir cologne. Aaron reclined in his desk chair with one Air Jordan perched on the wooden frame of his waterbed and a car magazine open in his lap.

He loved anything with wheels, just like our dad, and kept piles of those boring booklets by his bed. He'd flip past the pictures of girls in bikinis to the advertisements in the back. He could talk forever about subwoofers, *subs* in his lingo, which I gathered made the bass sound better, or louder, maybe. Rims too, which I learned went inside the tires. He wanted the ones that spun while the car was stopped for a red light. As far as I could tell, he hadn't made any upgrades to his black two-door Ford Escort since Dad had brought it home for him.

"What's up, kid?"

"Nothin.'" I wasn't ready to talk yet. Instead, I grabbed the open jewel case from the top of his dresser and nudged out the insert. I sat cross-legged on his carpet with the Green Day pamphlet in my hands and slid my finger across the lyrics while it played on his boombox.

I always felt incredibly cool to be listening to the same music as my big brother. He had lots of cassettes and CDs I could sing along with: Radiohead, 4 Non Blondes, Edie Brickell, Blind Melon. When I rode with him in his car, he blasted rap tapes, ones with a *Parental Advisory: Explicit Content* sticker on the front. We listened to Eazy-E, Too $hort, and Snoop Dogg. I didn't know all of the words, but I knew *indo* was another name for weed, and *gin* was what my dad said Grandma drank at Christmastime.

"Check this out," Aaron began once the song ended. "I'm in homeroom, right? And this guy wants to buy a tab off me."

"Huh?"

"A tab. You know, acid. LSD?"

I crinkled my eyebrows. I knew LSD was a drug, but I wanted him to explain it. He would always answer my questions if I bugged him enough.

"It's a drug that makes you see things. If anyone ever offers you some, you gotta say no, aight?"

I nodded.

"Seriously. You'd hate it, kid. Trust me." He held his eye contact for a moment to emphasize his point before continuing. "So, it comes in a liquid, right? And they use a dropper to put it on these little squares of paper that you put on your tongue. I keep a sheet of them in my notebook."

The fact that he used LSD didn't surprise me by that point. I had been gradually learning that Aaron pursued forbidden activities. Back when Mom was alive, he'd walk me to the Forty-Second Street overpass and make me wait there alone while he went into the convenience store across the street. Later, he admitted that the clerk sold him cigarettes even though he was twelve. Now, in the summers when Dad and Cheri were at work, we'd sometimes sit together atop the monkey bars at the edge of the backyard and talk. One day, after leaning from the jungle gym and spitting brown into the grass, he told me he chewed tobacco. My young mind filled with the nauseating pictures of diseased mouths I'd been shown at D.A.R.E. in school. He tried to squelch my concerns with nonsense that I mostly believed. *If I was gonna get cancer, I already woulda'. Some people just ain't susceptible.*

"So we transact," he continued, leaning forward now, his Nikes firm on the floor under his swivel chair. "We're cool, and then he says real loud, 'You got an eight ball?'" He looked at me, and after a pause added, "I guess you don't know what that is, either?"

"Yeah, I do! You shake it and turn it upside down, and it tells you Yes or No."

"Hah, naw, kid, that's a *magic* eight ball. What I'm talking about is, well, it's an amount of cocaine. An eighth-ounce, technically, hence the term *eight* ball. Aight, so he says it so loud, the teacher hears, right? And I can see from the corner of my eye" —he pointed then to the outer edge of his right eye—"that he's lookin' at me, waiting to see what I'll say next. But I think fast. I get all innocent. And I'm like, 'What's an eight-ball?' Saved my ass."

I exhaled, relieved to learn he'd avoided trouble. "How do you know the teacher knew what that was?"

"Oh, he knew."

I desperately wished he would simply follow the rules like I did. We were different that way.

One afternoon a couple of summers before, not long after I'd learned about his secret chewing tobacco habit, I rode with him to a routine doctor's appointment. In the empty stairwell on the way up to the second-floor office, he stopped, pulled the small can from his waistband, and held it out to me. I was terrified to hide it for him. What if I got caught? Wouldn't I be in trouble with the police? When he realized that neither my girls' jeans nor small hands could conceal the contraband, he removed his baseball cap, folded it around the tin, and demonstrated how to hold it in my lap. Of course I obliged—I idolized him—but not eagerly.

After Aaron disappeared with a nurse behind a door, I sat stiffly in my chair too close to half a dozen waiting patients. My heart pounded and my skin sweated while I focused on holding the folded hat just so. I pictured a pair of stern uniformed police officers walking through the door and asking, *What's that in your hand?* I was thrilled when he emerged half an hour later and motioned that it was time to go. The moment we were alone again in the echoing stairwell, I insisted he take it back. He was utterly relaxed as he replaced his items and suggested with a smirk that I *take a chill pill.*

Like those moments on the monkey bars and in the doctor's office, this glimpse into Aaron's world was both frightening and exhilarating. My shoulders squeezed toward my ears as I imagined him suffering the worst possible consequences of his risky behavior. And yet, I felt special to be trusted with his secrets.

A song later, when I was ready to shift the topic to what had prompted me to knock on his door, I moved up to the corner of his waterbed. I said in a low voice, careful to not be overheard, "I'm so sick of Cheri."

"You and me both," he responded, then turned the page.

"Guess what she said?"

Aaron looked up from his magazine but didn't put it down.

"Dad gave me money so I could go to the mall. And she was all like, 'Mike, she's a spoiled brat. You need to stop treating her like a princess.' Whatever! Like she doesn't spoil Melissa?"

Most days, I delighted in Melissa's company. It was fun to have a little sister, and by then I even occasionally got away with bossing her around. We played Tea Party with her miniature Tupperware set, candy-coated chocolates, and soft drinks. We played School with pretend worksheets, and Bank with her grandparents' old spiral-bound book of tear-away checks. With love, I came to call her my sister, dropping the *step*.

But I battled ever-present jealousy.

I envied her walk-in closet, chock full of Barbies, coloring books, and dress-up clothes, even more than I envied her and Aaron's street-side windows. I had wanted that room, but Cheri insisted that Melissa needed the space for all of her toys. More importantly, while her relationship with her mom didn't have the warmth of those affectionate lesson-giving *Full House* exchanges, it was infinitely more than I had.

"Hah, yeah. Five years old, girl doesn't even wipe her own ass."

I let my voice rise to mimic Melissa. "Mahm! Come wipe me!" It was fun to team up against her.

Aaron joined in. "Wipe me, Mom!" We both cracked up, and I calmed down. He was a sponge that soaked up the stress that splattered out of me, refusing to remain contained. Nothing compared to the satisfaction of being in his presence. As long as I had him, I knew I'd be okay.

"Guys, dinner!" Dad called us from the bottom of the stairs. I leapt up, knowing he'd be mad if we didn't come right away. I turned to make sure Aaron was following me. He was still sitting in his chair.

"Aren't you coming?"

"Yeah, in a sec. Go on."

I ran down the steps and around the corner into the bright kitchen. I took my spot at the far side of the oblong table, my bony back unrelaxed against the wooden spires of the chair. Cheri was taking baked potatoes out of the oven with a purple potholder I had woven. Standing next to me, Dad grabbed the biggest steak on the tray with silver tongs and put it on his plate.

Before he could give me one, I asked in my sweetest puppy-dog-eyes voice, "Will you cut mine for me?"

"What, you can't do it?" he teased with a grin.

I smiled back at him. "Not like *you* do it!"

Dad squeezed a slab in his tongs and added it to his plate before taking his seat to my left.

He always sliced my steak for me. Cheri still retells the anecdote that I thought I hated steak when she first met me, until she suggested my dad cut it for me. He could change the chewy chunks into thin, almost see-through slices I wasn't capable of creating myself.

Sitting in her chair across from me, Cheri cut tiny pieces of meat and scraped them onto Melissa's plate to her left. Then, leaning toward her daughter, she cut up her potato. Dad took a bite so big I didn't know how he could chew it, or why he didn't cut his steak the same way he cut mine.

Having just vented to my brother, I was in a relatively happy place. And when I was happy, I was talkative. I liked to share whatever recent happenings were on my mind, assuming my audience would be just as interested as I was. With my left leg folded beneath my butt to give me more height, I bounced in my chair as I talked between bites.

"I got a hundred percent on my spelling pre-test," I started.

They didn't say anything.

I explained what I'd learned a *hypothesis* was, and how we were doing experiments in science class to test our hypotheses.

They didn't ask me any questions, but they never did, so I kept talking.

I told them that the science teacher's pet rat was still hanging out in our classroom, and that he looked so cute when he picked up food with his two front paws and nibbled on it.

Melissa smiled at that, but our parents simply kept eating. That the image of a tiny adorable creature eating like a human didn't impact them was too much.

"Guys," I said loudly, looking back and forth between Dad and Cheri. "Are you listening?"

With a brief glance up, Cheri retorted, "Mandy, you talk just to hear yourself talk." Then, to my dad, she spat, "Are you gonna deal with your son?"

No one else at the table seemed fazed by her words, but I felt like the wind had been knocked out of me. I silently scolded myself for getting into the situation. I should have kept my mouth shut so she wouldn't have anything to comment on. It was my fault that I was hurt. I stopped bouncing in my chair and ate the food on my plate, pretending I was calm.

"Aaron!" Dad yelled, and my shoulders scrunched up at the sound. "Get your ass down here!"

Cheri lifted the bowl of sugared strawberries from the center of the table and added some to her plate, then Melissa's, before passing them to me.

A bit later I heard the stair rail creak, then Aaron was in the doorway. Without turning around or even lifting her gaze from her plate, Cheri announced sarcastically, "Nice of you to join us."

Aaron slid into his seat between Melissa and I without responding. He grabbed a foiled potato, unwrapped and squeezed it, then began covering its surface with slivers of margarine.

The conversation was light, with Melissa telling us about a game she played at recess and the guys talking about some Nascar race. I kept quiet to avoid the pain of another insult when tears were still so close to the surface. When Dad and Cheri shifted into planning errands, Aaron leaned toward me and whispered, *"Check this out."* He had the conspiratorial look I recognized from the many times we'd schemed about how to get under Melissa's skin.

Cheri didn't believe in everyday sibling rivalry the way it had been with Aaron and I when I was younger. When she caught one of us bullying Melissa, no matter how minor the upset, we'd be punished. So we had to be sneaky. Aaron was a master of finding ways to tease Melissa that wouldn't get us in trouble. A favored technique I'd copied was how he'd stare at her long enough to annoy her. She'd whine, *Mom, Aaron won't stop staring at me!* Then he could say, *What are you talking about? I just looked at you.* We also enjoyed letting her squeeze her little hands around one of our arms. *Doesn't hurt yet,* Aaron would taunt. She'd squeeze so hard her whole face would scrunch up. Then we'd laugh because it still didn't hurt, or at least it hurt so little I could pretend it didn't, and she'd be furious. Again, we couldn't get in trouble when *she* was the one trying to hurt *us.*

I wondered what he'd come up with that he was bold enough to try right there at the kitchen table with Cheri just two chairs away.

He pouted his thick lips, exposing the sliver of a melted ice cube, then sucked it back in, grinning. Then he turned to his right.

"Hey, Melissa, you know what a *loogie* is?"

"A what?"

"A loogie. You know, when you clear your throat and a bunch of phlegm and snot come up and out into a... like, a *booger* ball?"

Cheri tsked and crinkled her eyebrows. "Stop that."

"That's gross!" Melissa said.

"I think I have one coming." He shook his head, rubbed his throat, and wrinkled his face in worry as if preparing for some unwelcome bodily malfunction.

Melissa's eyes widened. "Don't!"

"Aaron, cut it out."

He cleared his throat, loud, just like I'd heard him do a million times before spitting into the grass. I wondered if he had changed his mind, if he really *was* going to spit out a loogie.

He stuck out his tongue, cradling the melted ice in its curve.

Melissa squeezed her lips closed and shook her head No.

Cheri tsked again. "That's disgusting!"

He smiled and pulled back his tongue, then jerked his head in surprise when the ice shot out of his mouth and onto Melissa's plate, right onto her half-eaten potato. She opened her mouth and bright pink vomit splashed onto her plate, the color of the strawberries she'd just eaten. Immediately, she started scream-crying.

Aaron laughed. "Calm down!" He tried to explain, "It was just an ice cube!"

I laughed with him and called her a baby.

Soon Cheri was crouched over Melissa. "You're fine," she promised. "Arms up." She lifted Melisa's white t-shirt off of her head and folded it so that the soiled Minnie Mouse print faced the inside. "Come on. Let's get you a new shirt."

Cheri stood and said to me, with a nod toward Melissa's plate, "Clean that up." They left the kitchen together. Dad headed for the back door, mumbling something about turning the grill off.

I sat for a moment, stunned by the quick turn of events. Why *me*?

"Get a bag," Aaron told me, nodding his head toward the cabinet where we stashed plastic grocery bags. "Naw, two." He walked across the kitchen for the roll of paper towels. I sighed in relief. He was taking on the nastiest part of the cleanup.

Maybe I couldn't rely on him, given his teenage priorities. But I could count on him to be more caring than the others in our household.

Two years later, alone in the chilly lowest level of our basement, I stood in front of the wall of shelves and looked over the boxes:

big plastic blue tubs, clear tubs, cardboard. Everything was labeled, mostly in Cheri's writing. But there were still a few with Mom's: black permanent marker on masking tape, crisped and peeling. I wondered how old they were and used my own age to do the math. I was thirteen, almost fourteen, in the middle of eighth grade. My mother died when I was seven, almost eight, in the middle of second grade. Therefore, I calculated a minimum of six years, and probably much older. I always knew which writing was Mom's. Her lowercase *e*'s weren't round like mine. They were more like a backward *3*: a dented little *c* with a straight line in the middle.

When we moved into that four-bedroom suburban house, Dad and Cheri argued about what to put in his china cabinet. Cheri didn't seem to want anything on display that had come from our lives before her. He won the debate over the two holiday plates Aaron and I had decorated in second grade, and even a metal plate stamped with Mom and Dad's wedding date. The bell collection got to stay with little argument, I assumed because she didn't realize they'd been Mom's, but more likely because their cut crystal sparkled. Everything else went into boxes that ended up on those basement storage shelves.

Besides the china cabinet, the only decorative elements in our house were Dad's antiques arranged atop the kitchen cabinets and Cheri's ceramic owls flanking a sofa. It was a large house with soaring ceilings, four bedrooms, and a big basement, and all of the walls were white and bare. When I asked if I could paint my room like my best friend had, Cheri, who worked in mortgage lending, insisted that you couldn't as easily sell a house if the walls weren't white. I wanted to hang framed posters, but she retorted, *Why would you put holes in perfectly good walls?* My first house had been cozy, adorned with framed Victorian-era art prints, gendered bedroom colors, and doilied table tops under endless houseplants. The home Dad and Cheri built together felt stark in contrast.

I lugged one of the boxes labeled in Cheri's writing (*Memories—Mike's*) onto the cold concrete floor. My back was to the old dresser in which we kept Aaron's extra clothes and car magazines. I expected him to come by and get them any day. I could hardly believe my parents had kicked my brother out of our house, an act I found inexplicably cruel.

Cheri had threatened to kick Aaron out countless times, generally after he roared insults at her. I didn't like the way she treated him. She made him yell like I'd never seen him do. She called him *a compulsive liar*. I got the sense that he did lie to her a lot, but he was more honest with me than anyone else was. First, she convinced our dad to send him away to a nearby boarding school, but he was expelled after stealing pink plastic flamingos from a teacher's lawn in the middle of the night. He enrolled in the high school half a mile away but skipped so often that he was failing. Cops charged him with *possession of drug paraphernalia* after finding a bong in his car at a traffic stop. He was punished so often I couldn't keep track of his offenses. The final straw appeared to be stealing a few hundred dollars from Cheri's sock drawer, money she'd been saving to take an Arizona vacation with a girlfriend. He was seventeen years old when she finally won the argument. This was when I learned she could get anything she wanted.

At first, he moved in with our maternal grandma across town. But she had kicked him out, too, so he was living in a hotel. I hoped he wasn't using hard drugs. He'd recently told me over the phone that he'd tried meth. One of our dad's friends had hired Aaron to help with a big painting job and suggested they get high in order to move faster. They stayed awake for days working side-by-side in an unoccupied suburban tri-level, ultimately meeting the client's deadline. Aaron told stories that way, as if every messy decision had a tidy justification.

I knew meth as one of the worst drugs, up there with heroin, mostly from the dark posters on the walls at school. The prospect of him becoming a sick and desperate addict terrified me. So, I tried to believe that it had been a one-time event. My brother wouldn't do meth twice, I figured; he was a smart guy. I boxed up his story like I boxed up my love for him, and I limited my agonizing glimpses inside to moments like this one, alone in the quiet, within reach of the chest of drawers that held his belongings.

I flipped the cardboard lid upside down on the floor, using it to hold what I removed from the box. I was afraid to let a trinket roll away and be found later by Dad or Cheri, who might scold me for going through their stuff. They didn't understand why I'd want to be in this cold corner of the house. When asked, I'd be evasive. I didn't want Cheri to crinkle her face, judging me as strange. I didn't want Dad to be upset by me mentioning the unmentionable.

When I got to the first brown photo album, I put it in my lap.

Dad had bought those albums on sale somewhere so he could organize all of our pictures. Even though they were ugly, I was excited. We could sort by year, I thought. We could label the albums. Insert paper slips to separate trips from special events from holidays. Then, I'd know exactly where to find the best pictures. Like the Polaroid I took of Mom, Aaron, and my cousins the night before she went to the hospital, the last photo ever taken of her.

I was beyond frustrated when I realized that Dad's interpretation of *organized* was nothing like mine. He extracted photos from small albums, envelopes, and the bottoms of boxes and threw each into the next available sleeve. Period. Now teenager Aaron was next to teenager Mom. The dozen photos of our neighbor's wrecked race car were spread across three separate albums.

I questioned him about it. *Well, I couldn't have worried about that*, he answered. *It would have taken forever. But they're all in albums now. No more loose photos!*

Above me, I heard a sound, so I tilted my head and listened. Dishes clanked together. I heard the boring noise of race cars going around and around a track. Having confirmed that I was still alone in the basement, I let out a breath.

I opened the album and flipped through it, stopping at a photo from an early family vacation, before I was born. It wasn't a very good picture. Dark. Mom and Dad smiling in a pickup truck. Nothing but grass outside of the truck windows. Dad had a mustache and shaggy black hair. He looked different but the same: his round freckled cheeks like mine and those familiar gray-blue eyes. Mom looked beautiful with her hair long, wavy, and parted down the middle, a style that disappeared soon after the portrait in which she donned a white nurse's cap, having graduated with an associate degree in medical assisting. Relatives so often said I looked like her, but I didn't yet see it. Maybe in her blue eyes, or the shape of her chin? I wanted to know everything about that picture. I wanted to know where they were and where they were going. I wanted to know that they loved each other. They *looked* like they loved each other.

I flipped quickly through a few pages of yellow grass and rocky hills. Then, a family photo from Grandma's dining room. I was six, standing with Mom, Dad, Aaron, and Mom's whole side of the family. We were clustered together between the dining table and a cabinet where new toys in boxes were piled precariously, like mid-game Jenga blocks.

We'd been going to Grandma's on Christmas Eve for as long as I could remember. We used to take a family photo every year using the delay timer on my uncle's impressive camera. He'd push a button and rush over to crouch in front of us before it flashed. We'd run through the routine a few times in case someone's eyes were closed, or because Aaron had stuck out his tongue. But Grandma made us stop after Mom died. I couldn't help myself from noticing who had passed away since that last Christmas photo was taken. I counted two dead faces: Mom and Grandpa.

At Grandma's house, this same Christmas photo hung in a gold frame above her couch. Once, I asked her why she kept such an old picture on the wall. She said, *Because it's the last photo ever taken of our family.* I knew what she meant: our full family included the people we'd lost. I missed how life was before, too. But it hurt my feelings nonetheless, her words implying that our family no longer existed—that she and I weren't family.

I slipped the Christmas photo back into its sleeve and flipped the album page, hoping for more pictures of Mom. I saw my cousins and me opening presents. Then a blurry, older photo of a big brown and black dog. Monster? It was one of the dogs they had before I was born. The next few pages showed Dad and Aaron at an automobile race together.

Then, I finally happened upon another good one: a picture of our family of four. Mom had short permed hair and large glasses. Dad still had shaggy hair but no longer a beard or mustache. Aaron was a little chubby with a buzz cut. I was a cute five- or six-year-old grinning in a pink windbreaker, sitting on a green dinosaur statue as if it were a horse. Aaron posed with his arm around me, and we both grinned as if someone off-camera had just hollered, *Say cheese!* I knew by the dino that we were at Flintstones Bedrock City in the Black Hills of South Dakota.

The four of us often took summer road trips. They blended together in my young memory: a collection of thrilling venues I could have visited once or half a dozen times. There was Wall Drug, where we got colorful candy sticks and tubes of flavored honey, and The Corn Palace, an entire building constructed of ears of corn. Aaron and I loved the Cosmos Mystery House, where you could stand up straight but look like you were tilted. At Bear Country U.S.A., wild animals came right up to our car window. I remembered stopping to look at Chimney Rock in the middle of nowhere, happy to see something Dad said was special, even if I didn't quite understand what made it so. We hadn't been on a road trip in years; Cheri hated them. She blamed something called *car sickness* that I was sure was made up.

I stared at the photo trying to memorize the lines on Mom's face, frustrated by its tiny size. I wished the photographer would have been standing closer. Did he need to get our legs and feet in the photo, and all of that sky? And what had we seen there besides that green dinosaur statue? Who took this picture? What did we eat for lunch? I looked up into the dark, cobwebbed corners of the storage room, as if reaching into the corners of my memory to clear the blurriness, but I couldn't remember anything about that day.

I looked down again at the four joy-filled faces. Dad was the only other person left in our house who was a part of *this*: what I secretly considered my real family. When our good moods overlapped, I enjoyed spending time with him.

I often accompanied him for Saturday morning errands while Cheri and Melissa slept in. We'd stop at a home improvement store where, after getting everything on his tiny scribbled list, he'd peruse the clearance shelves with glee. I'd roll my eyes while he tossed deeply-discounted items into the basket that I couldn't imagine him ever needing: fishing line, cabinet hinges, tiny tins of rejected paint colors. At the end of our trips, after filling up his truck's gas tank, he'd hand me the receipt and make me calculate his mileage. A change in gas mileage could indicate an engine problem, he had taught me. I didn't mind the routine; I liked the challenge of mental math. On the short drive home, we'd list off everything we had accomplished. *And look*, he'd say, pointing at the dash. *It's not even ten yet. What do you wanna bet those guys are still in their pajamas?* I'd smile. *Yep! Cheri's drinking her coffee, and Melissa's probably on the couch staring out the window.* I couldn't understand how my sister could enjoy simply sitting and watching people. I was always occupied, crafting or reading or watching TV. We were doers in my family.

Maybe my adoration of my dad was typical and inevitable. Or maybe it was intensified by our shared suffering.

"Mandy!" I heard Cheri's voice bellowing from somewhere far away.

I let out a grunt in annoyance, rolling my eyes dramatically even though, and especially because, no one could see me. I wanted to yell back (*WHAT?*) but not enough to risk punishment. My legs were starting to hurt anyway. I tossed everything back into the box, slid it onto its spot on the shelf (with the label facing the front, just like it was before), and hustled upstairs.

Cheri was no longer in the kitchen but stood in the living room pointing the remote at the TV. She turned toward me as I stepped up through the open basement door into the hallway, breathing heavily.

"What were you doing down there?" she asked as the screen went silent and black.

I shrugged. "Nothing."

"Well, hurry up. Your brother's on the phone."

"He is?"

I hadn't heard his voice in so long. I had tried to call him a few weeks before, but I got a recording of a woman saying, *You have reached a number that has been disconnected. If you feel you have reached this recording in error, please hang up and try your call again.* I did hang up and try again like she said, but I got the same message.

I ran into the kitchen and grabbed the receiver from where Cheri had left it on the floor. I tried to not sound out of breath as I greeted him. While we exchanged hellos, I walked around the corner and sat on the second-from-the-bottom step.

"So where are you now?" I asked, staring at the springy white telephone cord, taut against the wall.

"I'm in Delaware."

"Delaware?" My heart dropped into my stomach. "Why?"

Aaron launched into a story filled with things that surprised me, but he said them all as if they were no big deal. He met a girl at the hotel he was living in. Now she's his girlfriend, and he went all the way back to Delaware with her, where she's from.

"Why was she here?"

"She had to go out there for some legal stuff, to win back custody of her five-year-old daughter."

"How old is *she*?"

"My age. A little older? Twenty, I think." I did the math in my head and wondered why she'd want to have a kid when she was still in high school. He continued. "So anyway, I got a job welding. It's aight. I basically fix the machinery in chicken processing plants. We have cattle in Nebraska, right? Beef cows?"

"Yeah?"

"Well, out here they have chickens. You can't drive half a mile down the highway without running into another chicken plant. It's wild."

I didn't know what to say.

"So what's new with you?"

I shrugged my shoulders, then remembered he couldn't see it. "Nothin."

"How's school?"

"Fine." I wanted to tell him about my crush sneaking vodka to school in his bag, but I didn't want Cheri to hear. It was the kind of story I used to tell him in his bedroom, hoping to engross him the way he did me. I lowered my voice to almost a whisper. *"Guess what this guy brought to school."*

"You gotta speak up, kid, I can barely hear you."

My heart sank. "Nevermind."

"Okay… Your grades still good?"

"Yeah."

"Dad and everybody good?"

"Yeah, I guess."

We were both quiet then. I tried hard to think of something to say, but my mind wasn't functioning at its best.

"Aight, well, I guess I'll catch you later then?"

"Okay." I scolded myself for failing to sustain our conversation.

After I hung the phone up on the kitchen wall, I ran up to my room so I could see him. I closed my bedroom door quietly. I kept my favorite picture of Aaron taped to the mirror on the back of the door. It was from the previous Christmas Eve when he was living with Grandma. I had cut off the sides that held my little cousins' laughing faces, so Aaron was the only person in it. He wore a dark green polo shirt and looked back at the camera, surprised. I had followed him around the whole day trying to get a picture without admitting that I wanted a picture.

I stared at the photo up close and reimagined our conversation happening face-to-face.

Get this. This chick wanted me to go with her back to Delaware. Crazy, right? But I told her, naw, I'm stayin' right here. I've missed you, kid.

The pit in my stomach was turning hard as a rock. He was gone, gone. I was alone for good. I needed to know where Delaware was. I went to my closet and flipped through the stack of papers and books on the shelf until I found my United States map. I unfolded it on the carpet and leaned over, looking through all the state names on the right side until I found it. *There.* Delaware was a tiny state on the East Coast. I looked at the size of Nebraska, the stretch of paper from Omaha to the panhandle where I knew Chimney Rock stood. Then, I compared this to the distance between Omaha and Delaware.

It was very far away.

Why did he want to be all the way out there? I felt the pit in my stomach traveling up to my throat, threatening to come out. I didn't want to cry. I wasn't a baby. So I told myself it was no big deal. He'd come back soon. His girlfriends never lasted very long. Besides, he was just my brother, right? He had his friends; I had mine.

I carefully refolded the map and tucked it back in the closet where I couldn't see it. I blinked away my tears, smoothed my face, and went downstairs to watch TV.

No one understands me.

From a shoe box that once held a pair of pewter flats, I lifted my mom's dainty gold watch. It was a quiet autumn evening two weeks after Grandpa Dawn's death. Desperate to touch the few objects still in my possession that had touched my mother's skin, I had wandered down to our basement storage room to rifle through my boxes of her jewelry. I knew from the wear on this watchband that she had fastened it on the tightest setting. Wrapping it around my own petite wrist, I pictured her with me now: just a mother and her adult daughter swapping accessories.

Crouched on the concrete, I rubbed the soft leather backing of the Indian seed bead medallion she had stored among her simple necklaces, a piece I'd fiddled with as a child but had never seen her wear. Its texture transported me to the patch of carpet in my mom and dad's bedroom where I must have sat so often, between the two dressers whose matching mirrors could create an endless tunnel of reflections, as Aaron once showed me. It was a spot where I would have been out of Mom's way as she moved about in the morning from the bathroom to layer on her liquid foundation, to the edge of the bed to pull on panty hose, and to the narrow closet to select a skirt and a high-necked polyester blouse.

I lifted the pair of dangling gold and black earrings, wild as a lion's mane but light as a feather, from the lavender-gray velvet jewelry box. I remembered sitting in my spot on her floor and suggesting she wear them to work. Holding the physical evidence in my hands, I could be sure the moment had existed even if its details were remarkably blurred. I could almost see her warmly declining my seven-year-old enthusiasm in favor of modest studs. I could almost feel the way we loved each other.

I realized, staring down at the earring in my palm, that I was in one of my cycles again. This happened from time to time, generally in the months between my mother's October birthday and her January death. I'd think of her more and more often, and it would grow into a desperation to reconnect.

Several weeks earlier, I had listened to a spirit medium on the radio on my way into work, heart pounding with belief and envy. I contacted the station to request an on-air reading and was crushed to learn that her waitlist was more than three years long.

Around the same time, I emailed a local nonprofit to inquire about grief support events that might be well-suited to my situation. The employee who replied invited me to an upcoming support group for young adults. Most of the members weren't grieving an old loss like me, she explained, but I would still be welcome. Their next meeting was tonight.

After glancing at the time, I boxed up Mom's jewelry and headed upstairs to grab my coat and purse. Then, I drove across town full of hope. Sure, I was nervous about going to a new place, doing a new thing, meeting new people. But I was excited, too. I remembered facilitating an adolescent grief support group a couple of years before and the powerful connection those kids felt with each other. What if I could have that now? What if I could finally be my whole self in front of a group of peers who truly understood what I was going through?

What if this was the very help I'd been looking for?

I had been increasingly erratic. I went to bed early, snapped at Bob when he tried to be affectionate, and teared up at innocuous work emails that I read as personal attacks. Sometimes I sent Bob vengeful journal-like midday emails in which I defended the idea of quitting my job. *Have you talked to your doctor about quitting?* Bob had replied, referring to my therapist, Mary. *If you haven't, I hope you consider it.* I didn't know what he thought she could do. It's not that I was troubled by something specific to the job. It's that I was getting fed up with suppressing my depression for eight hours a day. Meanwhile, regardless of the nurturing of my therapist and support of my husband, I felt utterly alone. In one such email I wrote, *I feel like there isn't a single person on this earth who I can be completely myself with. I feel lonely, and I feel lost, and I need help, and I don't know where or how to get it.*

Maybe this was that.

When I pulled into the organization's parking lot, I had butterflies in my stomach. Something felt off. The building was a little too dark; the lot, too empty. But I'd sent the email confirming my intention to attend; I'd driven all this way. Surely they were inside and I was overreacting, like usual—letting the worst scenario play out in my head.

I slung my purse over my shoulder and walked toward the entrance. There I found a Scotch-taped sign fluttering on the door announcing that the session had been canceled due to a coming storm.

Canceled?

I stood staring for a moment as it sunk in that everyone else must have been notified, but not me. I swallowed a lump in my throat as I imagined why they wouldn't have contacted me. Did they not want me in the group? I hustled back to my car against the cold evening wind, my shoulders up to my ears and my eyes directed at the ground.

That weekend, I leaned against my headboard and scrolled through Facebook on my phone. The city lights funneled in faintly through the barely-open shades, but the double-pane glass did little to dampen the loud, cheerful voices of passersby. I was irritable and wished I could shake the sense of desertion that had stuck with me since the canceled grief support meeting a few nights before. A voice in my head mocked, *Quit being a baby!* I clenched my jaw, controlling a muscle since I couldn't control anything else.

On my tiny cell screen I saw family portraits with cute kids playing among burnt orange trees, everyone donning perfectly-coordinated flannels and sweaters. I saw selfies of my acquaintances dining on a Mexican beach at sunset, posing cheek-to-cheek with a chiseled husband, or laughing with a mom and sister under an artificially chipper caption about gratitude.

Fuck you and your gratitude. I fumed. I didn't trust people who had easy, trauma-free relationships with their parents and siblings. There was so much they didn't know. Meanwhile, my brother couldn't even send me a simple letter.

Though therapy had provided some relief, I still felt broken. So I had reached out to my brother hoping he could solve this puzzle. Aaron knew better than anyone else what being me was like. He, too, had lost Mom and lived with Dad and Cheri. There was, of course, the minor obstacle that we hadn't communicated in years. An awkward phone call had seemed like torture, and he wasn't good with email, so I sent a typed letter.

I told him that I had started seeing a therapist for depression. I asked, what did he think could be the reason that I was so emotional? Maybe he formed a theory long ago of why I ended up abnormal. I also asked him what he remembered about growing up with our mother. I had a nauseating desire to recall our everyday routines. I asked what we did on the weekends, what we talked about during dinner, and why I didn't remember Dad being around much.

I pictured a many-paged response in the same slightly messy print I read in his letters sent from prison and rehab a decade before. His vivid stories would fire off new connections in my brain. He'd turn my six- and seven-year old grainy freeze-frame memories into high-definition feature length films. Or, at least into home videos clips. Maybe his insights could benefit me more than therapy by helping me pinpoint the root cause of this problem. Just like with software bugs, knowing the root cause would reveal the solution.

I told myself that this was all I needed to fill the void, preferring the perceived safety of the mental realm to the unknowns of the emotional one.

When I slid the letter into our mailbox a month earlier, I felt excitement fluttering in my belly. I was sure that after years apart, I was going to reconnect with my first best friend again.

Now, I had waited and waited. Still, a reply hadn't come. I couldn't believe how lazy and self-centered he was being. What was so hard about writing me back?

I had checked in with my sister-in-law, Leigh-Anne, two weeks back, using the news of our step-grandpa's death as an excuse to reach out. I tossed in a question about whether Aaron had seen my letter as if it was an immaterial afterthought. She responded that they'd lost the mail key but she'd be sure to tell him, a story I found believable but frustrating.

It's not that I expected Aaron would solve all of my problems with a response to my questions. But it would help. Plus, I had hoped he would be as interested as I was in rekindling our pen pal relationship. The least he could do was tell me what he remembered about Mom. I had confessed to having depression, didn't that count for something? Did he really not care enough about me to do this one simple thing?

I worked myself into a fury aimed at Aaron and his apparent disregard for my feelings. From the bed, I thumb-typed a one-line email to Leigh-Anne:

I'll just assume Aaron no longer gives a shit about me since it's too fucking hard to write or call his depressed little sister.

I didn't sign my name. I hit send, slammed the phone on the window sill beside me, and headed to the kitchen. Regret set in immediately. A crying session with Mary earlier in the week had helped but clearly not enough. Why did I let myself hope that it had? I had suspected since childhood that I was unfixable. It was probably true. And now these stupid, unjustified emotions were making me be an asshole to people I loved. I stood at the counter and scraped out bites of hard cinnamon ice cream. Each melted on my tongue, delivering a tiny boost of comfort before dissolving into dissatisfaction.

A few days later, I settled into my desk at work with my first cup of bitter coffee and checked my personal email account. Leigh-Anne had responded.

Not that I'm trying to make excuses for Aaron, she wrote, *but he's been really withdrawn for some time now.* She mentioned unpaid speeding tickets, avoiding friends, and drinking more often. *He is on this emotional roller coaster and has said to me he's ready to get off, he's ready for the universe to take him away, which scares the hell out of me.*

I thought Aaron's depression had been fixed? He was supposed to be five and a half years ahead of me. *I know he wants to talk with you, and he's even worked on a letter, but I think he's afraid he'll hurt you more than help.* I narrowed my eyes with resentment at that line. What could he possibly say that would hurt more than *this*?

It's tough for him to talk about your mom. In fact, he's not even told me about the contents of the letter, but I figured it out due to his behavior. Please don't give up on him. It may not happen today, probably not tomorrow, but I swear he will get back to you. It's just really hard for him, but he loves you very much... If you ever need me, please call. I love you.

On the one hand, I felt relief. I had needed to hear that he loved me, that it wasn't indifference that had kept him from responding. On the other hand, I felt shocked to learn that Aaron was having suicidal thoughts.

Sometimes you hurt too much to see that everyone else hurts, too.

My stomach clenched. I wondered why he didn't just get help. He knew about the value of therapy; he'd seen counselors as part of his rehab program. I didn't consider the financial cost of mental health care, something that would be more difficult for a formerly-incarcerated blue-collar father than for me.

My mind wandered back in time to my own suicidal ideations, the ones that started as a persistent prayer for death around eight years old and disappeared by the time I graduated high school. I shivered in my desk chair against the frigid office air. I guess Aaron's urges never faded away like mine had. Mine *had* stopped, hadn't they?

Where exactly was the line between everyday malaise and the kind of hopelessness that makes you want to end it all?

I would need to toughen up to not end up where Aaron was, yet a mess after all of these years. He was still doing whatever Leigh-Anne meant by the *behavior* that gave away the subject of my message—freaking out when Mom came up, I assumed. I remembered hearing about the time his anger was triggered when Leigh-Anne had brought home Christmas decorations. An argument somehow escalated to him punching his fist through his own windshield.

Anger revealed itself then as a knotted jumble of stabbing wire tangled in my gut. I held it there because it felt so wrong. I was supposed to be empathetic. For God's sake, my brother was truly suffering. What kind of monster could be mad at someone in that situation? Me, I guessed.

This was an anger I'd been resisting since Aaron first left me some fifteen years before. As my life careened forward, I always intended for that anger to stay put. But it continued to eek out in undesirable ways, creating tiny stab wounds in the people I loved.

As I tamped down my fury, my mind toughened around this new reality. Aaron wasn't going to help me, at least not anytime soon. I wouldn't get to read his lengthy recollections about our life with Mom and his wise, thoughtful theories about my emotional struggles. I was on my own yet again.

I held in my grief, both because I was at work and because that's just what I did.

On the drive home after a counseling appointment with Mary, I tried to dream up how to combine the few items in our fridge and pantry to make something that might resemble a meal in five minutes or less. We were out of frozen pizza. I considered serving leftover quinoa and canned beans with my garlic stir fry sauce, but I didn't want to have to peel garlic. And plain soy sauce didn't seem appetizing. *Maybe I could eat cereal and Bob could fend for himself,* I thought. I had made it through a whole workday and another therapy appointment. I had earned a break from cooking, I reasoned.

When I opened our front door, I smelled food, and my shoulders dropped with relief. I put down my things, helped Bob set the table, and slid into the smooth fiberglass shell chair across from him.

"How was work?" he asked, opening a bottle of hot sauce.

"Fine. Got some stuff done. You?"

"Good. Lots of meetings, though. Oh, speaking of, how was your appointment?"

I set the plastic guacamole-dotted lid of my pork burrito bowl upside down on the table runner. Before my session, I had been wondering how one went about breaking up with a therapist. Whether I could send an email and just be done with it already. The problem was, I didn't have any clear reason to quit, just a vague desire that recurred every time I drove to her office.

Gratefully, that day she had given me what I considered a valid cause.

"You won't believe what she said." I paused and leaned forward for dramatic effect, then continued, "'There, there.'"

I waited for his reaction.

He took a bite of his burrito and chewed.

"Babe. I'm not exaggerating!" I reached my hand across the table and placed it over his. With downturned eyebrows I repeated in exaggerated theatrical sympathy, "'There, there.'" I shook my head. "That woman's a trip."

"Other than that, was it good, or…?"

How is he not getting this?

"No, not really. You know how the guys at work were being dicks the other day when I had to present?"

Bob nodded. I recounted the incident to him the day it happened. I had been asked to present some slides to Mark, Dan, and my two peers in a room we hadn't met in before. I went to the front and looked around for a way to connect my laptop to the projector. I fumbled with the various cords trying to find one with an end that might fit into one of my work laptop's many ports. Everyone remained seated, staring at me. Dan made a sarcastic comment about how tough it is to use computers, and Mark laughed. I could hardly believe no one even attempted to offer me help.

"So I told her about it, and she was like,"—I switched into my *poor baby* voice—"'Oh, yes, of course. How hurtful they are! No wonder you're feeling insecure.'"

On the one hand, hearing her normalize my internal experience provided some relief. They were being hurtful, and it was okay that I felt hurt.

On the other hand, I'd known since my first weeks on the job that they could be insensitive. Plus, I'd been depressed on-and-off for as long as I could remember, well before this job. While the presence of pain might have been excusable, the vastness of that pain didn't match up with the workplace exchange that had triggered it. Hers was not the revelation to end all revelations, as her satisfaction seemed to imply. Something was seriously wrong with me, couldn't she see that?

Of course, I wasn't particularly direct about any of this with Mary. I wanted her to diagnose me on her own, convinced that too much honesty would bias the results of her analysis. I was paying her hundreds of dollars, and I expected answers. If this was the best she could do, it wasn't good enough for me.

"That's what you said the other night, right?"

I rolled my eyes. "Well, yeah, but… That's not, like, *all* that's wrong with me. She acted like this was some huge discovery. As if *obviously* I'm depressed because these guys are jerks."

"Okay."

"Who the hell crawls into bed after work because their boss said something mean?"

"I don't know."

"Exactly! Anyway, I'm done with her."

"With her specifically or with therapy?"

"Ugh, would you stop? I'm gonna do something. It's just, I'm telling you, she's not good. She's just not." *And she said I could call to schedule my next appointment, so I'm pretty sure I got away with avoiding the breakup conversation all together.*

"Okay," he answered.

I sat in silence, my jaw clenched even while I chewed bland bites of beans and rice. It seemed apparent to me that Mary didn't get it. Bob didn't get it. No one understood me. Even my brother, who understood me better than most, wasn't available. I was going to have to rely on myself yet again.

I had always felt like I had to be self-reliant as a kid. It wasn't only that my emotional needs weren't met. It was that my stepmom leaned on me to soothe her emotional turmoil, too.

8 THEN

I can't be angry.

I sat cross-legged atop my comforter, a pastel print I found obnoxiously childish.

When Aaron moved out, I inherited his bigger street-facing bedroom, including most of his furniture. Cheri bought me a new bedding set after I complained about the crusty spots I'd found on his blanket. Knowing nothing about the bodily excretions of teenage boys, her quick action didn't satisfy me. I felt only frustrated by her color preference.

I slipped my newest letter out of its white envelope, which was hand addressed by my brother. He'd been living in Delaware, a universe away it seemed, for two years. For most of that time, we hadn't spoken. Then, a few weeks earlier, he'd started writing me letters from a correctional center.

His explanation of why he was incarcerated was nonspecific. He had written, *This girl I know got all mad at me and lied to the police. She basically tried to set her old man up, but I got suckered into it.* What did any of that mean? I assumed the truth was drug-related with some poor anger management mixed in. I had heard about him getting into fights at school and seen him yell fearlessly at both Dad and Cheri. As usual, he blamed his *dumb luck.* Since I was old enough to remember, I watched him break rules, receive punishment, and then point fingers, as if his life was happening *to* him rather than being the result of his choices.

Now, my brother and I were pen pals. I replied to each letter the same day I retrieved it from the mailbox, and I would have a response from him the following week. My dad knew about Aaron's incarceration and our notes but gratefully didn't ask what they said. It wasn't that anything in them was particularly secretive. It was that they were mine.

Our heart-to-hearts via paper and over geographic distance were like a drug: urgently satisfying and never enough. They lifted me somewhat from the loneliness I felt at home, where I didn't feel fully relaxed with either parent.

Most of my negative interactions with Cheri were subtle. When my first period came, for example, I went to her with a question. *It's brown*, I started. Though enthusiastic that it had finally happened, I was anxious about the color I'd found on my maxi pad that evening. With a grin I saw as a smirk, she replied, *You think it's bright red when it comes out of you?* I had, but I was too hurt to admit so. I never asked her another biological question, relying instead on health class and my friends' mothers.

My strained relationship with Cheri was exacerbated by teenage hormones. Our most heated arguments ended with me screaming in defiance, *You're not my mom!* followed by her grounding me to my room for several days or weeks.

While Cheri attempted to discipline me, my dad let me get away with a lot. Grandpa Dawn responded to my behavior more than once with an incredulous, *I'd never get away with speaking that way to my father!* But sometimes, perhaps once a month or so, the rules of engagement changed. Sometimes, when only our immediate family was around, my typically joyful and sociable dad transformed into someone furious and reckless with his words. I knew the warning flags like I knew my own reflection: flushed cheeks, a sulking toddler's protruded lower lip, and an illogical demand in a raised voice. If his anger was aimed at me, I might be summoned to, say, examine a tiny speck of dust in the corner of the room that I had missed when cleaning. But usually, his target was his wife. He insulted her body size and yelled about perceived household responsibilities she hadn't completed. Unlike the careful, passive approach I imagined my mom would have taken, Cheri fought back with equally hurtful words. He became a *chauvinistic pig* and a man who she *should'a never said Yes to*. When disagreeing about parenting, a favored topic, Melissa and I were thrown around the conversation as *my daughter* and *your daughter*.

As I unfolded the pages of Aaron's latest letter, these were the phrases that drifted through my cracked open bedroom door. Our parents were downstairs fighting again.

When Aaron lived at home, his presence cushioned the blows of this tension. I could escape into his room, an entirely different world in which we spoke at normal volumes and listened to each other. It was a world of such inconsequential topics as the rims he hoped to buy for his Ford Escort.

I focused on the page and read, *I learned to drive when I was ten.*

I'd been practicing driving for nearly a year, since turning fifteen the past February. Despite weekly lessons with my dad in his pickup truck, I still had little confidence. Nothing about maneuvering a motor vehicle came naturally to me. Though I'd had no accidents, I'd made half a dozen mistakes that I knew *could* have been accidents. Once, at a stop light near our house, I'd hit the gas pedal when meaning to hit the brake. My dad assumed I hadn't seen the light, and I was too embarrassed to say otherwise. When pulling into a parking spot at Target, I tapped an adjacent car, gratefully not leaving a mark. I changed lanes on the interstate without remembering to check my sideview mirror and blind spot.

In my last letter to Aaron, I'd complained about my poor driving skills. Reading his bold claim now, I remembered him telling me that our mom had let him drive for his paper route when he was twelve. The details of this story were becoming more dramatic. He enjoyed storytelling as much as our dad did, and while I never felt lied to, I was sure they both exaggerated. Like how Aaron once bragged to me about going to a No Doubt concert. The story kept getting bigger. Not only was he there, he was in the front of the crowd. Not only was he in the front of the crowd, but he reached his arm up over the edge of the stage and touched Gwen Stefani's famous abs. I continued to read.

I started with permission with Mom in Dad's white 4X4, in the snow, on my paper route on Sundays. And I hung out with people who were older than me, so I was playing designated driver when I was thirteen. It'll come to you. Concentrate on the basics. It took me a few wrapped-up vehicles to learn the control at the edge, and how to bring it back from the edge. I've studied a lot about the physics of traction, momentum, force vectors, and all that get around a turn fast mumbo-jumbo.

For once, we were not on the same page. Wrapped-up vehicles? Control at the edge? My goal was to not hit another parked car.

Aaron also wrote about his young daughter who had been born about a year after he left. He shared the words she was learning and that she was the reason he had been ready for rehab. *The important thing is to get this shit done and over with and tend to my duties as a father.*

In an earlier letter, he'd said he wanted to move back to Nebraska soon because he believed the schools were better. I'd asked him when. *You'll get to see her, don't sweat it. I'll work on it. I'd like to be out there before she starts kindergarten, but first grade is really a priority.* He switched pens to one with more black ink. *If I'm still on probation, then I'll have to try to get it transferred and so on. But I'll do what I can.*

I paused to imagine his homecoming, something I did often. I pictured us sharing a freshly painted two- or three-bedroom midwestern apartment while I attended college, spending weekends playing with my niece. I moved my half-asleep legs to lie on my stomach and willed myself to focus on the page rather than the arguing that continued downstairs. Toward the end of his letter, Aaron's writing became so vulnerable it was as if he was writing for no one to read.

It's pretty crazy knowing I might spend a year in this place. I'm one of those people who just can't function without a hug from someone I love every so often. I hope I make it. Right now is the first time I've cried since I've been in here. But I got to let it out sometime.

He was crying at rehab? My torso twisted in worried knots. What if someone caught him? Would they beat him up? And what did he mean by, *I hope I make it*?

"I'm getting a divorce," I heard my dad threaten. "You better pack your shit." This empty threat was so commonplace I only rolled my eyes. I didn't understand why they got married when they seemed to hate it so much. I heard the garage door rumble open beneath me and then creak closed on its track. I heaved a sigh of relief. He had left, and the shouting was over for now. I knew he'd be back later that night. Tomorrow he would do something nice for Cheri and otherwise act like nothing strange had occurred.

Moments later, I heard my stepmom call my name from downstairs. I stayed in my room and hoped she wouldn't say it again.

"Mandy, could you come down here?" She was trying to make her voice sound relaxed, but I could tell she was crying.

I took the steps slowly. The living room furniture was rearranged to accommodate our illuminated faux Christmas tree, which stood tall in the center of three front windows off to my right. Cheri sat on the loveseat, facing the stairs from which I descended. Days before, the couch had been flipped one-hundred-and-eighty degrees and pushed just past the loveseat to face the tree.

Once on the first floor, dread rose in my gut as she motioned for me to sit on the couch near her. I didn't want to be with her. I wanted to be alone in my room. I was still amped up from all of their yelling. I boxed up my stress where, at least for now, it wouldn't get in the way of the pretending I had to do.

"I just–" she inhaled quickly, "don't understand what your dad expects from me." She held a wadded up tissue in her jittery right hand and wiped it down both cheeks. I sat stiffly on the couch where I was supposed to.

"He can be such a jerk," she sobbed. "He walks all over me. I'm not a doormat. I don't deserve to be treated like this."

I nodded and relaxed my face into what I hoped was neutral. Unreadable. My insides twisted with painful empathy. I hated to see her cry. And at the same time, I was pissed. Cheri was on her third husband, as my dad so often pointed out, so in my mind it was clear who the problem was. I was unwilling to see any similarities between her and my mom's relationships with my father.

She whined, "I don't have the money for a divorce. I don't know what I'm gonna do."

I zoned out, trying not to hear what else she said, because the more I listened, the more I wanted to argue. I sat silently while she vacillated between shades of sadness and anger. Eventually, she was taking deep breaths and gradually relaxing. I let myself calm a little, too. If I could just keep my mouth shut, I'd be able to go back to my room soon without consequence.

After a moment, she cleared her throat and sat up taller. When she spoke again, her voice was strong. "Your father doesn't know what it's like to be married."

Excuse me? My stomach twisted tight, fury replacing all remaining pity.

"You know, I knew your mom in high school."

I braced myself, breath held, so I could take whatever she was about to sling without reaction. The only time I remembered her mentioning my mother was to mock the eye makeup she wore as a teen.

"She chased your dad around like a lost puppy." She shook her head. "She did *everything* for that man. For Christ's sake, if he said jump, she'd say how high."

How dare she bring my mom into this? How dare she claim to know anything about our family?

"Well, I'm not like LuAnne," she went on. "If he wants to stay married to me, he's gonna have to get that through his thick skull."

Fuck you, I shouted in my head. While Cheri looked at the tissue in her lap, I imagined grabbing her shoulder-length hair in my fist and dragging her to the carpet. My muscles tensed as I pictured kicking her in the stomach until she'd beg me to stop: *I'm sorry! I swear, I'll never insult your mom again!*

Instead, I kept my face as relaxed as possible and waited to be excused.

"Mandy, honey," she put a hand on my knee and tears filled her eyes again. With a wobbly voice she continued, "Don't you *ever* let a man control you." She took a breath. "Tell Melissa I'll be up in a minute."

Finally, I thought. I went straight to my room and disappeared in the comforting quiet and blackness under my covers.

In that moment, as with many others, I felt as mad as my dad and had no idea how to handle it. I saw what anger expressed looked like for Dad, Cheri, and Aaron. I wasn't willing to face the consequences of treating my immediate family that way. At school, though, I could get away with being mean, the worst punishment being an occasional half-hour detention. I'd long had a bad habit of making fun of girls who were even less popular than me. I'd mock their speech impediment, heavy weight, or unshaven legs. In eighth grade, it escalated to a phase of yanking on a classmate's ponytail through English class. I didn't like her nasally voice, her wide masculine gait, or the ease with which she laughed loudly with friends. As if addicted, I couldn't resist my urge to hurt her. I liked being the creator of pain. I liked how powerful I felt when she failed to uncurl my fingers from around her dark brown strands. In the years since, I've felt remorse about tormenting those girls. But at the time, I left those interactions feeling neither satisfaction nor guilt. I felt hollow.

Perhaps most stressful was that I wasn't allowed to tell anyone about my parents' loud arguments. I chose to break this rule carefully by confiding in my closest friend. Kelly was a smart, compassionate girl in my grade who lived a block away. We shared nearly all of ourselves with each other. I once answered her questions about my mom's death when sleeping over in her pitch black basement, our tears dripping onto the spare mattress. Now, I couldn't wait to get to school the morning after one of these incidents and find her in the hallway before homeroom. I'd recount every turn with as much drama as I could create, racing to the conclusion where I knew some semblance of release awaited me. Kelly's downturned eyes, her clumsy words of consolation: they were treasures I tucked in my pockets and carried with me throughout the school day. I swore Kelly to secrecy which, as far as I ever knew, she kept. Of course, being children, we never got very far in the quest to understand our guardians.

Once Aaron was released from rehab, our letters ended. Communication dwindled to annual Christmastime phone calls to our parents' house. Those conversations were clumsy. I didn't know what to talk about. If I complained to him about the cranky owner of the small grocery store where I cashiered, would I sound petty? I was sure Aaron didn't want to hear about my little problems when he had a toddler and a rocky relationship with her mother to worry about. If I told him how thrilled I was to be narrowing down my college choice after earning multiple academic scholarships, would it be bragging? Aaron was off-the-charts smart, but because he skipped class so often, he left town one credit shy of a high school diploma. Wouldn't my talk of higher ed be cruel?

Beyond the calls themselves, I didn't know how to handle the maelstrom of emotions they churned up. In contrast, my dad didn't show any evidence of struggling. Embarrassed and self-critical, I armored up. I would come out of my bedroom, return the cordless phone to its charging dock, and go about my holiday business as if I was perfectly content to talk to my only brother for a few minutes once a year.

In reality, I missed him so much that I daydreamed about the high school secretary announcing my name in her boring voice over the speaker: *Mandy Partusch, to the front office. Mandy Partusch.* I'd get to the office, and my brother, catching sight of me, would stand up from the waiting area chair and casually stuff his hands into his sagging jean pockets. He was moving back to Nebraska and stopped to surprise me before telling anyone else. *What's up, kid?* he'd say with a grin.

I finished high school with no such announcement. I moved away and finished college the same. I always hoped to be at home when Aaron called on Christmas and asked for Dad, and I hoped not to be.

With each passing year, my faith waned while anger swelled silently. I hated that Aaron wanted to spend all of his time with his new family and none with me. He left me in a home that he knew was dysfunctional. Beneath the anger was sadness: maybe I didn't matter to him. Maybe I wasn't lovable after all. Then there was Cheri, who pushed him away, and Dad, who let him go. These were the people I most loved, but also the people with whom I was most angry. How could that be? My anger seemed wrong—unsafe. So I squeezed it into a dense ball and stuffed it far down in my torso, beneath the other boxed-up needs, where it would be rarely felt and never consciously acknowledged.

As best as I could, I forgot about Aaron.

9 NOW

I'll feel better soon.

I watched Tenth Street from behind the half-lowered shades of my chilly bedroom window, nervous-excited for my stepfamily to arrive. The buoyant city sounds of light traffic and occasional pedestrians trickled through the glass.

Ten days earlier, I had left Mary's office that final time with a lead weight on my chest. I didn't want to keep seeing her, but I couldn't bear to give up on myself, either. Feeling somewhat calm after two months of weekly therapy sessions, I decided to try a short-term service opportunity. I had volunteered in a variety of ways over the years. In middle school, I reshelved library books to meet my service requirements for Catholic Confirmation. I boxed up canned goods at the foodbank, tutored students after school, and, after college, mentored an underprivileged girl. I wanted to experience what I loved most about volunteering: the sense of altruistic accomplishment and distraction from my cycling self-centered thoughts. Plus, I wanted proof that I could follow through. I had the discipline, but did I have the emotional stability? I was certain I could as long as the cause wasn't too close to my tender heart, like the children's grief support group I facilitated a couple of years before.

Ever efficient, I had found something that served two purposes. I signed up to bring six dozen cupcakes to an upcoming Big Brothers Big Sisters holiday event. It gave me a low-commitment volunteer gig, plus I could pair the activity with inviting my stepfamily to our new condo.

Over the gray shades, I saw my aunt Denise pull her SUV into a spot across the street with Grandma Mary in the passenger seat and my teenage cousin in the back. As their doors and jaws opened and closed, I craned my neck higher as if it would help me hear their conversation.

At Thanksgiving, I got the sense that Grandma wanted to be invited to our new place. *I haven't been to that part of town for ages*, she'd said. *You know that Dawn and I got married at the Sokol a few blocks from there?* She'd mentioned, *I don't have much going on these days. Course I'd like a reason to get out of the house.*

"Come on in!" I greeted, opening the building's heavy glass door before they could start bumbling with the keypad. Cheri and Melissa had pulled up, too, and were close behind on the sidewalk.

Keira joined us in the landing, hopping on her front paws because she was too obedient to jump onto our guests but too thrilled to be still. My stepfamily wasn't dog-crazy like me and mostly walked past her politely. Melissa, however, stopped with a smile and treated her to affectionate pets.

"I always forget how big she is!" She had a lap-sized fluffy Pomeranian.

"Yeah," I replied. "She's so happy to see you."

Why was it so hard to voice that I felt the same?

Once everyone had settled inside, I pointed out the supplies. In preparation, I baked seventy-two chocolate cupcakes, whipped up a big bowl of white buttercream frosting, and bought an assortment of Christmas-themed sprinkles. We got to work.

"Oh my god, that's so cute, Denise!" I gushed at my aunt's cupcake art, a mix of piped icing and well-distributed red and green jimmies. "You're such an artist."

Denise used to live next door to her sister. I remembered walking through the front yard to her place during the summer we lived in Cheri's little yellow house. Shirts would be spread out on the kitchen table, puffy paint drying around iron-on designs.

"Hah! Yeah, right."

"Your cardboard fish got us to second place," I argued playfully.

Everyone in the room smiled knowingly at my reference to the summer flotilla contest at Grandma and Grandpa's lakeside cabin. We used to spend the weekends leading up to July fourth in the hot but shaded garage, painting giant pieces of cardboard cut from appliance boxes. The year I referenced, our theme had been *Under the Sea*. Denise had the creative vision to cover the sides of Grandpa's pontoon boat with blue tarp dotted with ocean creatures. I sewed myself a green sequined mermaid fin and laid on the back of the boat. Her stepson, Ryan, strapped a homemade shark fin to his chest and followed us on a black inner tube. The two other old-enough kids, Ryan's sister and Melissa, smiled and waved from the front of the boat as we passed our audiences: families lined up in the sand on beach chairs.

"That was a good year," she agreed. "Remember Ryan's sunburn?"

Cheri shook her head. "That boy," she laughed. Unbeknownst to his caregivers, he hadn't put on sunscreen. His bisque skin was lobster red by fireworks time. "That shark fin was so cute, though."

The conversation carried on like that, a continuous stream of lighthearted recollections and harmless family gossip. But while everyone remained friendly on the surface, I was minor freaking out inside. I never felt at ease around this crew. I smoothed buttercream onto cake while holding the weight of old resentment in my shoulders.

When they left, I let myself sink into my bed for a minute thinking, *Done*. Then I lifted myself up and went about the rest of my evening numb to my surroundings and myself.

When I woke the next morning, I had an unexpected emotional hangover: I was sad.

Bob and I had agreed to go to the Holiday Carnival together and work a morning volunteer shift. I no longer wanted to go, but I had made a commitment. Not to mention, I had a countertop full of cupcakes that were destined for families who had much harder things to deal with than I did: incarcerated dads, long hours at low-wage jobs, or a recently-dead parent.

Toughen up, I commanded myself.

By the time I was showered and dressed, Bob still hadn't budged from his side of the bed. I stood near him and saw that he was awake.

"Will you kill me if I don't go with you?"

Why does he do this to me? I seethed.

I foresaw how embarrassed I'd be to show up alone after promising that two volunteers would be there to help. I hated his willingness to do exactly what he wanted. But I didn't want to be a nag like I perceived my stepmom to be. I wanted to appear easygoing and comfortable with letting him make his own choices.

"No," I answered flatly.

"Sorry."

Really? Or did you know from the moment I asked you that you weren't gonna do it? It wasn't a weekend activity he'd pick, I knew. He liked to stay up late and sleep in. He liked to have his Sundays obligation-free. But I also knew that if he just went, he'd have a good time. He lit up around kids, and they lit up around his focused attention. Plus, he had made a commitment to me, and I was hurt.

As he closed his eyes and his mouth slacked open again with deep edge-of-sleep breaths, I made my decision. I'd go, but I wouldn't be happy about it. I'd be quietly angry.

By the time I parked my car at the venue, the lump in my throat and churning in my stomach clarified that I wouldn't be able to fake it for my volunteer shift. I couldn't be energetic and smiling from the moment I walked in the door, as I imagined was required.

Inside, I asked the first person I ran into, "Excuse me, do you know where I should put these?"

"No, sorry."

I asked everyone I saw until, finally, a chatty woman led me toward a big classroom with tables set up in the back, already crowded with unstackable desserts. After dropping off the treats, I kept my head low as I retraced my steps down the school halls, eager to get out of there without a concerned staffer noticing my distress. Just one last thing to do before I could enjoy the private interior of my car.

I found someone standing tall with a clipboard, looking more in charge than the others.

"Hi," I said while silently planning the words that could get this over with the fastest.

"Hi, there!" she greeted me loudly. "Here to volunteer? What's your name, honey?"

I swallowed. "Mandy Kubicek, but, I'm sorry, my husband's not feeling well. I need to get back home." It wasn't a total lie.

"Oh, I'm so sorry to hear that. I hope he's okay?"

I pretended not to realize that she wanted to deepen our conversation. "We had a two-hour shift at ten," I said, moving my gaze from her to her clipboard in hopes of leading her gaze there, too.

"You said 'Mandy'... Oh, yes, I see you."

"Thanks." I turned away and hustled out the double doors. Within moments, I was back on safe territory, sipping black coffee from my thermos, relief having lowered my shoulders. *Done.*

On the drive back to my neighborhood, I wallowed in self-reproach. I told myself that I was selfish and unreliable, less generous than others, less capable of follow-through. I told people I'd be there, that I'd add value for a change, and then my obnoxious feelings got in the way. Yet again, I failed to be of service to people who actually needed the help.

When I got home, I strode inside, pretending that nothing unusual had happened. An undercurrent of emotions swirled in my body, and I didn't want anyone to know.

Bob was surprised to see me. "You're back."

"Yep."

On top of everything else, now I saw him standing in our kitchen with a calm expression holding a steaming mug of his beloved flavored coffee. My fury over him abandoning me that morning rose to the surface. But to bring that up would be an overreaction, wouldn't it? I didn't want to yell like my parents did. I didn't want to speak if I couldn't be clear and organized, and that feat felt impossible.

Bob didn't push the subject. He probably didn't want to trigger my wrath.

I watched the laptop screen as Bob scrolled through Netflix, looking for a movie. We sat side-by-side, him in the cushioned office chair and me in the turquoise shell chair he'd dragged into the office from the dining room.

In our last home, a forty-plus-inch flat screen hung on the living room wall beside the fireplace with our couch centered across from it. When we bought this condo in September, we debated where to hang that TV. It only made sense on one of the walls in the open living/dining/kitchen area, but we both wanted to watch less of it. We had slipped into sometimes eating dinner on the couch, staring into its glow. So, we sold it, committed to trying life without a true television set for a bit. Having to watch from a laptop definitely reduced my consumption, but not as much as I'd hoped.

"I'd watch *Eternal Sunshine* again," I offered.

"Yeah, maybe." He kept scrolling.

I remembered that movie being creepy. *Erasing memories every time you're hurt by something?* I thought with a shiver. *I'd have no memory left.* I was reminded that I'd been meaning to find a new therapist, someone I might trust more than Mary. Since I still wasn't able to volunteer without losing my shit, I admitted to myself that I could use some professional help. Plus Christmas was just around the corner, and I wasn't doing so hot with the pending deathiversary. But this was harder than choosing a dentist or gynecologist. I couldn't ask around at work or post the question on Facebook. I didn't know if my friends were seeing anyone, and how would I ask without sounding offensive? *Hey, you seem like someone who might see a shrink...?*

Bob scrolled further down the webpage, into older movies I imagined no one ever chose.

"I've been thinking about how to find a therapist."

"The insurance company has that website, right?"

"Yeah, but I don't want to just find someone based on location again. I guess... I wonder what's out there, you know?" I was thinking about the counselor I saw after I graduated from college and moved seven hours away from everyone I knew. "That lady I went to in St. Louis used hypnosis with her other clients. And I know what you think!" I preemptively rolled my eyes, certain he was judging hypnotherapy as nonscientific and therefore ridiculous.

"I didn't say anything."

"It's not like I want hypnosis. It just seems like a lot has been developed since Freud's days, and I want to know my therapist is up on all that stuff."

"Makes sense."

It would be really amazing if she knew about all *kinds* of things that can impact emotional health, not just the straight-up traditional therapy stuff. Like food. I remembered being frustrated by a Nurse Practitioner I saw once for my annual gynecological exam. She was concerned by the lack of cow's milk in my diet, not aware that many green vegetables deliver more calcium. I wanted a therapist who thought about health holistically. Someone who cared enough to study up, not just on new therapies but on healthy eating, mindfulness, and exercise.

"Maybe I can even find someone who's into, like, nutrition and stuff. Is that crazy?"

Bob shrugged, keeping his eyes on the screen. He switched over to TV shows. "People specialize in all kinds of stuff."

"Yeah. Anyway, that's my goal. And if not, I'll just find someone that looks decent. Maybe someone younger... but not too young?"

"Cool."

When Bob finally picked a show, a historical wartime series that sounded like a yawn fest, I told him I no longer felt like watching TV. I grabbed our second laptop and headed out to the couch, inspired to look for a therapist.

Later, I blinked forcefully to unglue my contacts from my eyeballs. When I looked away from the screen to rest my aching eyes, I squinted at the time on the microwave. I'd spent nearly an hour sifting through generic profiles and health provider review sites with no reviews.

I should give up for tonight, I thought. *I'll just check one last search term. I haven't tried* holistic *yet.*

Midway down the short list of search results, I was struck by a biography. *A psychotherapist who's into yoga?* I smiled.

There had been a quaint yoga studio near my St. Louis apartment that I longed to try but decided wasn't worth the cost. Bob, ever the problem solver, bought me an extra thick mat, canvas shoulder bag, and gift certificate. Still, I never worked up the courage to go inside, to contort my body into vulnerable positions with people I'd never met. I'd tried maybe half a dozen studios since then, never going more than once or twice. There was something about yoga that drew me in, yet every time I hit the mat, I squirmed uncomfortably and gave it up for another couple of years. I loved the *idea* of being a yogi: waking up every morning and doing sun salutations in my expansive, sunny living room like those toned women on YouTube. But I hated how, when I couldn't figure out a position, the teachers glared at me like I wasn't taking it seriously. Or they'd put their hands on me and reposition my body without asking for permission.

I kept reading: *Teresa continues ongoing study in Ayurveda, Chinese Medicine, Western Herbalism, nutrition, meditation, and Tai Chi.*

Nutrition? Meditation? I wrote down her name and phone number, and set myself a reminder to call when their office opened.

The next day, I breathed a sigh of relief when her office confirmed that she was taking new patients. She had an opening the following week, just before the new year. *Perfect.* I added it to my work calendar with a sneaky one-letter description: *T.*

I arrived early for my first appointment. The waiting room was what I expected: plain wooden chairs, low-pile carpet, and stacks of popular magazines. My fingers trembled as I flipped through a *Good Housekeeping*, ignoring the pages.

"Mandy?" she greeted with a warm smile. I recognized Teresa's bright blue eyes and dark blonde hair from her online bio.

"Yes, hi!" I set down the magazine, grabbed my purse from the chair beside me, and stood, hoping she couldn't detect the subtle shaking in my hands. What was I so nervous about anyway? I didn't have to tell her anything I didn't want to.

Once inside Teresa's small, windowless office, I glanced around. It was sparse, apart from a few things on the walls and a packed bookshelf. I was in awe, and a little jealous, of the range of emotional-health books: *The Gifts of Imperfection, Dialectical Behavior Therapy, Overcoming Trauma Through Yoga, A Course in Miracles, The Power of Now…* This woman seemed to seek knowledge from everywhere she could.

After sitting in the firm upholstered chair nearest hers, I noticed a Mason jar on the edge of the desk behind her. It was lidded and filled with brown liquid, dark lumps settled at the bottom.

"What's that?"

"Tea." She grinned at my perplexed expression. "I guess it does look a bit strange. It's an herbal blend I take for gut health."

"Cool." *Weird.*

Teresa wore her hair natural, with curls and waves poking out wherever they landed, and had no noticeable makeup. Her attire, however, was by-the-book business casual: khaki pants, a pink cotton button-down, heavy brown lace-up shoes. The disconnect between their rigidity and her down-to-earth energy was like the paper dolls I used to play with. Their paper outfits had paper tabs that folded over shoulders and around waists, never quite matching the form beneath.

Teresa grabbed a folder from her desk and moved it to her lap. I read from the empty upside-down form on top: *Treatment Plan, Goal, Objectives.* My chest fluttered. I loved the language of goal setting.

Goals had long helped me get what I wanted in life. In college, I realized during a summer study abroad trip to Spain that even the dramatic and glorious change of scenery wasn't enough to resolve my doldrums. Back home, before the first semester of my junior year began, I committed to doing better. My two best girlfriends and I sat with markers and construction-paper cutouts to make posters. Mine had four meaningful focus areas: *perspective, attitude, friendships,* and *health.* Each area was supplemented with new habits, like reflecting on what was going well and working out at the University gym. As I took action that fall, the inner change was so profound that I finally attracted my crush. Just the year before, Bob had responded to my advances by telling me I was too stubborn to see romantically. So, the evening of our first official date was such a monumental achievement that my bffs followed me around my dorm room with a camera. They captured me beaming in a form-fitting lavender v-neck sweater and black circle skirt, my hair meticulously straightened, the poster visible over my shoulder.

"I like to write out your goals so we have something to look back on every few months. It helps me make sure I'm providing you with what you need. Would that be okay?"

"Sure," I answered nonchalantly. *Are you kidding me? Hell to the yes it's okay.*

Teresa asked me some additional questions, and I watched her scribe my desires exactly as I recited them. Then she handed me the form so I could confirm what she'd captured.

Presenting Problem: off & on recurring depression. Short-Term Goals: Increase understanding of the 'why' underlying feelings (especially self-doubt, sadness.) Develop more self-confidence. Increase emotional healing to move toward fulfilling her purpose.

As I read the completed form, my vision blurred, and I blinked away the wetness. Teresa was the fifth therapist I'd seen in my decade of adulthood, and none of the others wrote down explicit goals for our time together. Before then, my mental health needs were obnoxiously abstract, not fitting into the tidy boxes of goal setting. Now that a straight-faced professional had written down my wishes, making them tangible, I allowed myself to believe they were realistic. Maybe I wasn't forever broken. Surely she'd only record a goal that was possible to achieve.

Faith had been with me as far back as I could recall, even as a child when it looked like begging God to gift me with death. Now, it had brought me to Teresa's office. I didn't know what lay ahead, but I knew I could take one step forward, and one step after that.

Against the backdrop of goals captured in black and white, I expected a productive cadence. We'd be checking these objectives off as complete in six months or so, no doubt.

Next, Teresa asked me questions about my life situation. I told her about my history of on-and-off mild depression and my current work stress. I told her about my blended family. I mentioned, "My mom died of a brain aneurysm when I was seven."

"Mm. That sounds like a significant loss."

"Yeah, it was." *But it was forever ago,* I thought. *Can't be all that relevant, right?*

When it was time to wrap up our visit, I booked a session for the following week.

Teresa had a way of looking at me that was so... blank. Not cold, nor pitying. Rather, completely devoid of interpretation or judgment. Like she was a field of cool green grass, and I was a picnic blanket spread open.

I was hopeful. Again, I remembered the counselor who helped me in the winter following college graduation. I walked away from those sessions with my head held high and my heart softened. Because after fifteen years without my mom, we reunited.

10 THEN

I don't need to be nurtured.

I sat in the kitchen of my first apartment, a sunny one-bedroom near the sprawling green Forest Park in central St. Louis, Missouri. My table was topped in protective grocery store ads, and the stench of craft glue filled the room. Hunched over in the chair, I carefully adhered vintage floral fabric to the outside of a cardboard file box.

I had recently moved out of state for my first post-college job as a software engineer. Finally financially independent and hundreds of miles from my parents, I was excited by the freedom. Though I knew almost no one in the city, I enjoyed a long-distance romance with my then-boyfriend, Bob. He had remained in Nebraska to finish his degree but made the seven-hour drive to visit whenever he could.

Despite the excitement, I quickly learned that I was ill-prepared for the transition. With no one around for whom I needed to force an upbeat mood, I spent entire weekends in bed. I didn't know why sleep was so tantalizing, but I hoped a counselor could crack the puzzle that was my psyche. I had signed up for four sessions, free thanks to my company's Employee Assistance Program.

In our first meeting earlier that month, the therapist and I chose a relationship on which to focus. I had briefly introduced her to my childhood's cast of characters: my mom, my dad, Aaron, Cheri, and Melissa. She asked me, *Which of those relationships do you wish were better?* with a notebook open in her lap. I replied, *All of them.* As we narrowed in on an achievable next step, our conversation kept circling back to my brother. I missed him terribly; we hadn't spoken much since he moved away. The thought of improving our relationship was too wrought with fear, though. Instead, I chose to focus our sessions on Mom. I suspected her death was still impacting me. Plus, she wasn't around to reciprocate, so it seemed the easiest place to begin. It was in our second session that the therapist encouraged me to make the Mom Box I was currently decorating: a special container of mementos that I could sift through regularly to help me process my grief.

While the box and lid dried on the kitchen table, I sat cross-legged on my scratchy tan bedroom carpet and sifted through a plastic tote labeled *Sentimental.* I was looking for my few Mom-related possessions and anything else from my life before that might bring happy memories.

I lifted out the squeaky-eared stuffed dog our neighbor had given me at Mom's funeral, then the brunette Cabbage Patch Kid she had bought me that Christmas. I squeezed the doll to my chest and sniffed her scentless scalp as if she were a real baby in a mother's arms. Nestling it in my lap, my left forearm across her chest and under her floppy arms, I grabbed the Precious Moments snow globe Grandma bought me for my First Communion.

I smiled at the memory. Bored one day at Grandma's home, I had opened the delivered package that held my future gift. Upon discovering me with the treasure, she scolded me, boxed it back up, and told me I'd have to wait. Soon after, while Mom was in the hospital and my First Communion was still a few months away, Grandma suggested we put it in Mom's room, which I thought a dandy idea.

Now, I held the faded snow globe in my right palm and re-read the inscription: *My Guardian Angel.* I flipped it over to watch the star-shaped flakes fall. As a child, I had believed that this dome of pastel plastic might save my mom. Somehow, beyond all reason, I still had faith in its magical powers.

I took the white teddy bear in a hot pink Peony Park t-shirt out of the tote. When I was six or seven, Aaron came home from a day at the local amusement park and handed it to me, along with an identical bear in purple that I gave away when we moved. *You have another one just like it,* Dad had asserted. I thought I could remember receiving those bear twins from my smiling, adoring brother, but had Mom told him to do so? Had he come home, perhaps having won them for a girl at school, and been forced to give them to me instead? No, I didn't want to think that. Besides, everyone knew that pink and purple were *my* favorite colors.

I set aside the two boxes of Mom's jewelry, her high school diploma, her Barbie and Midge dolls. I lifted out the few childhood books I had kept: the hilarious *Mrs. Piggle-Wiggle*, a hardback Care Bears volume my preschool teacher had inscribed for my fourth birthday, and a book of children's prayers. I placed an opened McCall's envelope on top. It held the sewing pattern for a unicorn costume she made me one Halloween.

I grabbed the cassette tape with a recording of Mom's voice that I'd once found among Dad's storage boxes. She had developed hand pain in her thirties, perhaps carpal tunnel or early arthritis, and experimented with sending her out-of-state sister, Patty, audio instead of handwritten letters. In the tape, she tells my aunt about putting our first dog down. At one point, my tiny voice appears in the background. *Can you tell your Aunt Patty what happened to Cinnamon?* Mom asks. Then, *Cimanon died,* a young me announces in a high-pitched, happy voice. I seem to leave the room then, or at least my attention does. *The kids were so upset,* Mom tells her sister through tears. *It was the hardest thing I've ever had to do.*

Scattered throughout the tote were Walgreens and Walmart envelopes of assorted photos. I sifted through them, making a pile of my favorites so I could add them to an album later. I organized the collection chronologically, from baby pics to the Polaroid I took mere hours before Dad rushed her to the emergency room.

That night, the night before Christmas Eve, my mom had babysat for her sister who was in town for the holidays. Aaron, as the oldest kid, hovered near Mom's side to help her manage the chaos of having a baby and toddler in the house. I was a chatterbox zipping around our small home, thrilled to have an additional playmate. *Shut up!* Aaron had hollered more than once. *You're giving Mom a headache.* At one point, Mom suggested I take a picture.

My crossed legs beginning to tingle, I stared at the photo taken fifteen years before. In it, my two cousins sat on Mom's lap in the wooden rocking chair, all three looking tired. Aaron squatted and smiled maturely beside them. I desperately wanted to see my mother as beautiful, but I couldn't. Her eyes had blinked closed, and her face was unnaturally pale from the piled-on ivory foundation she used daily. Her hair was short with overgrown bangs pragmatically bobby-pinned to the side, as one does for a busy evening at home. It was a habit I, too, would adopt in my thirties. On the side opposite my brother, I saw an end table draped in a white doily and an antique glass-front bookshelf. No less than three houseplants were visible in that one tiny corner of home. After Mom passed, we hadn't been able to keep many of her houseplants alive.

If she hadn't died, I imagined she would have given me her green-thumb wisdom. We would have walked through her house, a woman and her newly-independent daughter, discussing each varietal and its specific needs for water, sunshine, and soil. She might have sent me off to St. Louis with a few of her favorites potted in used containers that she found thrifting. She was a master of finding a deal.

I placed the photo gingerly atop the others. There was just one more item I wanted to include in my new Mom Box: the high school essay about her death. Because writing about a challenging time had been an officially assigned task, it seemed a reasonable excuse to dredge up those distressing two weeks between her collapse and her final breath. I was as ravenous for details as a gold miner rushing across the country. I culled my memory with pen in hand and even asked Dad questions, which he deflected. The writing had been a therapeutic, albeit primarily solo, endeavor. My teacher gushed over the final result and my confident assertion that *everything happens for a reason.*

At the time, I was a relatively happy eighteen-year-old. I had great friends, even better grades, and exciting plans for college and beyond. I knew that Mom's death hadn't destroyed me. On the contrary, the experience had given me gratitude for, as I wrote then, *the gift of life I was so graciously given.* In this way, it made me who I was: ambitious and brave.

Everyone touches tragedy at some point in his or her life, I had written in conclusion, long before I became conscious of the nonbinary nature of gender. *All we can do is move on and learn from our experiences. From telling people goodbye every time they leave to finally thanking God in my prayers, my mother's death has brought more than sadness to my life; it has brought wisdom.*

Back then, when I read the *A+* on a sticky note my teacher had stuck to the top of the page, the subject felt as settled as a hardbound book clapped closed. I had found meaning in her death, and a reasonable adult had praised my perspective. I was convinced that I'd done the work needed to come to terms with my loss. To grieve. To be over it.

And yet just days ago, when I told my therapist what it was like to lose Mom, I felt breathless trying to get the words out. I was utterly disappointed to be shown that I wasn't over it at all.

Once my Mom Box held everything I owned that felt relevant, I kept it in the front of my bedroom closet where I saw it every day. Sometimes, I'd sit at night and sift through its contents. If I was feeling numb, it might spark something. If I was sad, it would release the wellspring of tears, leaving behind a bit of calm.

Though my therapist had helped me some, I never fully bought into her schtick. I was turned off by the music she had me try, headphones streaming sounds meant to relax. Instead, the reduction in sensory access scared me. I was intrigued by her stories of how hypnosis had helped her clients integrate trauma and transform their present-day relationships. Not enough, however, to lay down and relinquish that much control. But placing mementos in a box? I could do that.

Several months after our free sessions ended, I lounged on my couch, pointing the remote at my small flatscreen TV. I flipped through the cable channels looking for something entertaining and paused when I saw a *Star Trek* rerun. I enjoyed watching the spaceship crew of *The Next Generation* outsmart aliens. More importantly, I remembered lying beside Mom in my parents' waterbed and watching *Star Trek* on their TV. I absorbed so few details of the show then that I had to confirm with my dad several years after her death, *Was it Star* Trek *or Star* Wars *that Mom liked?*

There was so little I knew for sure.

I enjoyed having my Mom Box, but I was frustrated that the compilation of mementos was an incomplete, if not inaccurate, reflection of her life. I hated that she died before I got to know who she was as a woman. I felt jealous of the people in my life who *did* get to know her: Dad, her friends, her siblings, and even Aaron. Our time together went too fast, developed in mere moments like the Polaroid I had been holding and staring at lately. I wanted the slow, satisfying experience of traditional film: the kind that took weeks to develop and you didn't mind at all because you had something to look forward to.

I wondered how I could get to know her better.

I wished it was easier to talk to my dad about her. He could talk for hours on end about anything. Often, it seemed, about nothing. Yet on the rare occasions that I brought Mom up, he'd manage to twist the conversation away from her. I never had the fortitude to steer it back. When he did speak of her, it was *Mandy's mom* or sometimes *my first wife*—never *LuAnne*. And when he needed to reference her death, he'd say with his characteristic crass humor, *She dropped dead.*

Dad! I'd shout. *Why do you have to say it like that?*

What do you want me to say? What else would you call it?

I'd shake my head, roll my eyes, and grunt in exasperation. *Not that!* He argued that it accurately described her sudden and unexpected death, but I hated that phrase. It reminded me of the obnoxious redhead from the movie *Drop Dead Fred*.

With no family nearby, I eagerly eliminated any face-to-face options. I wanted to get to know my mother without the added anxiety of navigating a real-time conversation. I thought Aaron might talk to me, but I hated the phone and didn't have his email address. When we were penpals for that brief but buoying period in high school, he once wrote, *I haven't talked to you too much lately. Every time I call, you don't really have anything to say.*

He was right. I preferred our letters. It was easier to plan what I wanted to tell him, to sit down and write it out, than to come up with something to say when I heard that strange Collect Call recording, then my brother's voice, out of the blue.

How can I explain my muteness? That was middle school and high school, the days of my first period, first liquor, first bong hit, and endless crushes. My days involved the stressors of constantly bickering parents and advanced mathematics courses I hoped would earn college scholarships so I could escape. And lurking in the background of this emotional unrest were a dead mom and a brother who had abandoned me.

The thing is, my little body trembled with so much suppressed emotion, responding skillfully to the sweet sound of Aaron's voice was an impossible ask.

While Captain Jean-Luc Picard stood speaking to a crew member on my television screen, I considered writing Aaron a letter and, my stomach churning, quickly rejected the idea. It had been ten years since we'd seen each other and several years since we'd talked. Then, Mom's sister came to mind.

My aunt Patty was the closest thing to Mom on Earth. Her frame was petite like my mother's. Her cheerful voice, reserved language, and blonde permed hair, all similar to Mom's. Plus, I had some fond memories with Patty. When I was in middle school, I traveled to Wisconsin with Grandma to spend two summer weeks with her, my uncle, and my cousins. She taught me how to crochet a granny stitch. I sat on her couch for days with the photocopied pattern page, meticulously looping variegated pastel yarn into a doll-sized blanket. She also bought me my first tampons, which Cheri had insisted I wasn't old enough to use. With one quick trip to the store and a brief how-to talk, Patty ended my recurring fear of one day walking up the stairs of my junior high school and having someone see a bulky pad under my clothes or a brownish-red leak on the seat of my khaki cargo pants.

These days, as with the rest of my maternal family, Patty's and my relationship seemed to thrive only in late December when holiday traditions demanded our reunion. I couldn't imagine surprising her with a phone call and asking my questions aloud. I wondered if a letter might work. Patty was kind of old-school; maybe she'd even appreciate the format. Besides, letter writing had been fruitful before with Aaron. Guilt pinched my shoulders, scolding me for not being brave enough to pick up the phone, and I ignored it.

That afternoon in my quiet apartment, the heart-warming memories of my letters with Aaron moved me to action. I gathered a pen and paper, sat at the kitchen table, and anxiously wrote my aunt a letter packed with questions about Mom.

What did Mom like to do? When she wasn't cooking, cleaning, or taking care of us kids, I meant. I shared my own memories of her baking cookies, teaching me to sew, and growing fruits and veggies in our backyard garden. *Did she like baking? When did she start sewing? What all did she grow?* I shared some of my memories of that terrible winter: visiting Mom in the hospital, coming home to a packed house and realizing she had died, going shopping with Patty to pick out the ivory scarf that would cover her shaved head at the funeral. *What do you remember about the end?* I asked. My aunt wasn't only an adult at the time; she was also a nurse. Her version of events was sure to bring different details than the ones I'd gathered so far in snippets over the years.

Less than two weeks later, I checked the mailbox after work and grinned as I grabbed what was inside: a thick amber envelope, my name on the front in Patty's slanted cursive handwriting. I bounced inside and plopped onto the couch to read her reply. It was an eighteen-page handwritten letter, packed with details and stories I'd never heard before, about Mom's joyful life and her death. My heart sped up as she covered the latter: describing that awful Christmas.

I told my dad I would drive, and he made me go through all of the red lights to get to the hospital. We got to her room. She was talking—here she had scribbled out what looked like the beginning of *not making any sense*, then wrote instead—*and in a lot of pain. They did a CT scan and found the aneurysm. They couldn't give her what she needed for pain because of the bleeding from the aneurysm. She looked miserable.*

My stomach twisted into a knot. *Pain.* Although it made sense, I hadn't realized that Mom was in agony. I didn't want to believe she suffered. I preferred to imagine a neutral end to her life, an easy transition from at home and healthy, to numb and unaware in the hospital, to dead. The concept threw me off balance, as if I were a teetering bowling pin. If I was able to block *this* from my awareness, what else was I blocking? I let warm tears fall down my cheeks and continued, ravenous for new information.

Two weeks later, when they took her to surgery, I prayed so hard. She had two aneurysms that needed to be repaired. They repaired one, but her heart rate kept dropping when they tried to fix the second. They weren't able to fix it. My dad called us and told me that LuAnne was braindead. I'm sure it was one of the hardest things he had to do.

Many of my memories of that time were physical: wounding stabs of pain rather than linear, logical visuals. But I did remember being taught that term, *braindead*. I remembered learning that Mom's brain had stopped working and a machine had to breathe for her.

By the time this word entered my second-grade vocabulary, I had seen her in the hospital at least twice. I didn't understand much, but I recognized that it wasn't exactly *her* I was seeing. I might have compiled and analyzed evidence, mentally making a trusty two-column list to help me suss out what was real. *Aaron called her Mom,* I would have noticed. One vote for *Still Mommy.* But also: *She looks at me like I'm a stranger.* A mark for *Not Mommy.* Or maybe I knew viscerally that the Mommy of my memory was gone. Either way, what did the terms *braindead* and *breathing machine* mean to me if I had already lost her? How did I feel?

I leaned over then as if pulled, like someone reached their fist through my belly button and was squeezing, twisting, agitating. At the blurry edges of my awareness, I recognized with shame that when my mom died, I had felt some *relief.* Relief that that stranger in the hospital, where my skin crawled like it was covered in bugs, wouldn't be coming to live in our house after all. Not-Mommy in Mommy's body, a monster as much as the terrifying blue horned man I watched crawl out from under the *Wonder Years* boy's bed in a scary movie. Nightmare avoided. And, at the same time, the devastation of nightmare realized: the real Mommy wouldn't be coming home, either. I closed my eyes and waited for my sobs to slow before I read on.

When we got to the hospital, I went to see LuAnne and cried. She had her head bandaged from the surgery, was on a ventilator, and had EEG electrodes hooked up to her scalp. I touched her hand and kissed her, but I knew she wasn't there.

My poor family. They too were devastated, and most of them hadn't been much older than my current age when it happened. It wasn't just my experience, but *our* experience. My heart warmed with compassion as I looked back for the first time through adult eyes. Through eyes that knew they weren't superhumans who had figured everything out, but people as vulnerable as me.

I needed to keep reading, but I also needed to take care of the sob-snot nearing my upper lip. I placed the pages on the coffee table, then rushed into the bathroom to blow my nose with toilet paper. Back on the couch, I took a breath and continued.

My mom and dad were beside themselves. Mike kept quiet mostly and tried to keep things 'light.' That certainly sounded like my dad, always cracking jokes when a conversation got uncomfortable. *LuAnne had agreed to be an organ donor, so we were to say goodbye so they could harvest her organs. We gathered around her bed, a priest said a prayer, and we individually said goodbye. That was the first time I saw your dad cry. He grabbed a paper towel from the sink to wipe his eyes and left the room. That was by far the most awful day of my life.*

Dad. My dad had lost his person.

My mind flashed to Bob and the potential of experiencing his death some day. I couldn't bear to imagine what my dad might have felt then as a young husband and father. Instead, I wondered what he did when he left the room. Was it back to business, to getting things in order for the upcoming funeral? When did he allow himself a fuller expression, tears like the ones I was crying now? Had he ever?

If he had, it wasn't in front of me.

I pulled my feet up onto the couch, laid my head on the scratchy side pillow, and cried. I would wait and put Patty's letter into my Mom Box after reading it one more time.

A few days later, feeling calm and refreshed, I returned to Patty's letter to revisit her stories of Mom's life. Stationed again at my two-person kitchen table, I cut pieces of cardstock and jotted down snippets of trivia. A mix of memories, stories I'd gathered over the years, and new details from Patty's letter began to supplement the pages of my Mom photo album.

Spent hours in the garden, I wrote in finepoint marker, *grew lots of vegetables, got asparagus to grow on the side of the house then killed it by putting ashes in the soil.*

I could remember Mom in the garden on a sunny day. We'd crouch down together with our faces close, our tennis-shoed feet on the grass just outside of the brick edging that surrounded her strawberry patch. Maybe she wore long gardening gloves. Or maybe she gardened bare-handed because she was tough. In my mind, she looked right at my eyes from behind her big plastic turquoise-framed sunglasses, and we smiled in unison.

Loved to cook, especially bake, especially desserts.

I could remember being in the kitchen, knees bent, peering through the glass of the oven door to watch her pie crust, fruit crisp, or cookies turn golden brown. I, too, enjoyed the magic of transforming powdery white flour, sparkling sugar, and softened yellow butter into delicious dough.

Sewed her own clothes—made Patty a box of Barbie clothes, made her dress for eighth grade May Crowning mass, taught me to sew a heart cushion.

I could see Mom and I sitting together at our antique oak dining table, her fingers expertly passing a needle under and over to show me how to turn scraps into a tiny heart-shaped pillow.

Supplemented with these details about what had brought her joy, my Mom Box finally felt complete.

This gathering process illuminated two inaccuracies I had unknowingly internalized. First, it was both normal and okay for me to have needs. I was only able to embrace this vital nurturing Mom Box practice once I felt self-compassion. Second, it wasn't just *my* loss. All of my mom's family and friends were hurt by her early and sudden death.

I've since come to see that no matter how alone we feel in our grief, even the most personal of losses are felt in community.

11 NOW

I'm a bad wife.

Dressed in my only pair of athletic shorts, a stretched out sports bra, and a cotton T, I stepped onto the front porch and squinted against the early summer sun.

My therapist had given me this idea. A couple of months into our sessions, we talked about my tendency to hold in my anger. I thought letting it out would mean yelling my venomous thoughts to whoever happened to piss me off. Teresa had some alternate ideas about expression. I could break fragile thrifted dishes into a big cardboard box, she suggested, or journal about my feelings, or exercise.

In middle school, I dreaded the *Presidential Physical Fitness Test* timed mile, so I was surprised when running piqued my interest. I'd run occasionally, not for fun but because it seemed like what I was supposed to do, particularly when on a weight-loss kick. The first time I went for a run with mental wellness in mind, I could only make it a few blocks from our condo before walking home deflated. But I kept putting on my running gear. Kept heading out the door, breathing a little more steadily, running a little longer. Now, I was training for my first race: five kilometers, or three point one miles. I was proud of myself for working up to that distance. I was even *enjoying* running, something I never thought would be true.

I started the running app on my phone, zipped it into the new sweat-resistant case on my left arm, and jogged down the sidewalk. I felt the cooling breeze of my increased pace against my cheeks and arms.

I was glad Teresa inspired this new routine, but after almost half a year of regular sessions, I still had mixed feelings about her. Sometimes, I felt safe and supported in a way I'd never felt before. Other times, doubt overtook me. Like the time she tried toe-tapping. She had me put my feet up on an extra chair, close my eyes, and recall a painful memory while she tapped two fingers against my shoe, alternating from left to right. I was *so* not into it, but I couldn't think of how to say No without being a bitch. So I sat with my eyes closed and pretended to remember something.

I thought often about quitting but miraculously had only canceled an appointment once. That was back when it fell on January tenth, the anniversary of my mom's death. I didn't know which of my feelings to believe. I'd been called gullible many times before. But, I'd also been criticized for not trusting people enough.

At my halfway point, a robotic voice alerted me from the phone velcroed to my bicep. I allowed myself a few walking steps, then headed back toward home at a steady jog. I passed by the boxy brick yoga studio I'd been eyeing since we moved, with its giant Buddha statue in the window and purple curtains always drawn. As I passed the brief strip of businesses that followed (a family-owned bakery unchanged for decades, a tiny recording studio, and a Mexi-Rican restaurant that always looked like it was just about to go out of business), I half-heartedly imagined going to a class sometime soon. I still felt both attracted to and repelled by yoga moves.

While I focused on the even pumping of my arms to distract me from the burning in my legs, my mind wandered to the question of whether I needed to keep seeing Teresa. Maybe I'd made enough progress for the time being. I had tools, like the cheat sheet I kept in a drawer at work. It had positive affirmations like *Everything is exactly as it should be*, and ways to cope when I noticed feeling overwhelmed: *drink hot tea, listen to music, do a non-work project for a bit*. I wasn't on the verge of tears every day like I had been, and I was getting better performance reviews. I was running. I had even booked another trip to visit my brother in the fall.

It had been four years since I'd flown out to see Aaron. My first visit to Delaware was an emotional reunion with Bob as my travel companion. My second and most recent visit took place just seven months later. My maternal grandma, my dad, and I traveled together to attend Aaron and Leigh-Anne's wedding. I remembered playing with the kids in the living room while keeping half of my attention on the adults. Grandma watched her great-granddaughters, the smile never leaving her face. Aaron and Dad stood shoulder-to-shoulder in the open kitchen area, looking at photos on a phone. Though their weights varied by at least a hundred pounds, they were mirror images in mannerism. They were both eager storytellers, comfortable with talking over each other. Each put a hand on the other's shoulder in the same way to emphasize a point. Aaron looked dressier than usual in a red polo shirt and hair styled with gel. Dad, too, had kicked it up a notch from his usual plain t-shirt to a white polo. I imagined him standing in his walk-in closet with Cheri days earlier and deciding what to pack. For the wedding, a suit and tie: easy-peasy. But what was the appropriate level of dressed-up to stop by your only son's house, a son you hadn't seen in twelve years?

That weekend, I watched our grandma watching Aaron and wondered what she was thinking. How did she interpret his black-spotted and missing teeth, or his thin frame? I wasn't sure what shape his teenage addictions had taken in adulthood. Leigh-Anne occasionally mentioned his drinking in our email exchanges. I smelled marijuana on my first trip to Delaware. But he always seemed present. My best guess is that, at least for the most part, he avoided harder drugs once he became a parent. What we witnessed were lingering effects. On the long car ride back to the airport, Grandma commented that he took after our lanky great uncles. I pretended to agree. Dad got home and wrote him a four-figure check for new teeth.

As my tennis shoes made drum beats on the concrete, I smiled. I was looking forward to my upcoming adventure, a family visit appended to a quick stop in New York City for an Ani Difranco concert with Bob. The last time I'd seen Aaron was about three and a half years before when he flew to Omaha for our grandma's funeral. It was definitely time to see him again.

While in this and many other ways I seemed to be doing well, it was also all so new. I feared that I wasn't as skillful as I thought, that I relied fully on our counseling sessions to keep me above water. If I took a break, I figured, I could get a sense for whether I could manage emotional challenges on my own, or if I'd drown. That seemed important.

Besides, if I was being honest with myself, it was hard. *We have to feel the sadness to move beyond it*, Teresa often said. I still wasn't so sure that reliving years of childhood upsets would be worth the effort. I was exhausted by all of the emotional presence. I deserved a break, didn't I?

I thought about how I could cut the cord with Teresa. I could say, *I'd like to take a break from this to focus on my job*. Or, *I feel good these days. I think this'll be my last appointment unless something comes up*. Maybe even, *I'd like to take a break for a month. Just take some time to process what we've talked about so far*. Yeah, that approach sounded promising. I could always go back in a few years if I wanted to do more.

My stomach churned. As with Mary, I didn't want to keep going, but I didn't want to be a quitter, either.

Close to home, the voice called out *three point zero miles*, and I slowed to a walk. The burning in my legs immediately cooled.

Once inside, I headed straight to the kitchen to chug a glass of cool tap water, then moved to the center of the living room to stretch. I stood facing the half-wall of windows opposite our kitchen. Beyond them, Keira lay stretched out on the deck in a patch of sunshine. I reached my fingers up to the ceiling, then down toward my toes, stretching the backs of my legs. In my peripheral vision, I saw Bob enter the kitchen and open the fridge, standing in its light with one hand on the stainless steel door. I pictured the cold air floating past him into the spaciousness of the room, the appliance's mechanisms working hard against the stress of the held-open door. Cheri's voice sounded in the recesses of my mind, *Close the fridge! You're wasting electricity!*

"What are you thinking for lunch?" he asked.

Suddenly, my mood shifted. My head was drowning in a pool of guilt-inducing thoughts for not having planned a lunch when meal planning was one of my only familial responsibilities.

I shouldn't have messed this up. I'm a bad wife.

Just as quickly, my shame turned to anger: fear directed outward.

Doesn't he appreciate that I'm taking care of my mental health? Why should I have to cook, anyway? Why do I always have to be the one to plan ahead?

I stood, my eyebrows tilted with contempt, and retorted, "How are you so completely unable to feed yourself?"

"I just, you know, if you had something planned... You don't *have* to cook."

I pictured Teresa. *Deep breath. Just notice*, I could almost hear her reminding me. I was a little dizzy from standing up so fast, my heartbeat was still elevated, and guilt squeezed my shoulders.

Deep breath.

My heart slowed, the feelings dissipated some, and clarity took their place. There was nothing to be angry about, I realized. Like he said, I usually cooked, so he wanted to check in before he prepared something for himself. It was an innocent, reasonable question to gauge whether I already had a meal plan for us.

And as for that guilt, I could still make it right.

I walked around the island to Bob, nervous for his reaction but nonetheless determined to eke out the two words that I had so much trouble saying.

"I'm sorry," I said, looking him in the eyes. "That was really mean. I don't know why I got so upset."

"It's fine."

I couldn't tell if he was being honest, or if he preferred to avoid further conversation. For the moment, I preferred not to know which. "I think I'm just stressed out about how much I need to get done." I had brought my laptop home to knock out some tasks without the typical interruptions of the workday. "I hate working on the weekend."

"Me too."

We embraced briefly, our wordless way of signaling the end of a conflict. "I'm gonna go shower."

Standing in the tiled stall, letting the wide spray of hot water meet my tight shoulders, my thoughts returned to therapy. All this *noticing* that Teresa was teaching me, and I was starting to recognize my emotions when I overreacted. There was a time when I wouldn't have been able to apologize and would have run off to bed instead. This was real progress.

And just like that, the optimism that was with me when I first met Teresa had returned. I was determined to keep showing up, to master this new model of strength.

I felt as proud as I did when I made the tummy-rumbling choice to visit my brother after eleven years apart. No matter how many accolades I had acquired, it was undoubtedly my greatest accomplishment. It transcended all other goals, both in the weight of the fears I had to drop and in the beauty of what I received.

12 THEN

My brother doesn't want to see me.

I lifted my head from the pillow and whispered in the dark of Bob's bedroom, echoey among the wood floor and soaring ceiling, "You awake?"

"Yeah."

I was twenty-four years old. After a year of long-distance dating, Bob received his undergraduate degree and moved down to St. Louis to join me. We were each renting our own first apartments, three miles apart. Though we saw ourselves getting married eventually, we valued the experience of living on one's own before trying to live with a partner. I slept over at his place frequently.

Now roused from slumber, Bob lifted his arm from around my t-shirt-covered torso and rolled onto his other side. I followed suit and spooned him from behind, wrapping my left arm around his belly and resting my fingers on a soft bed of curly hairs. This had become our evening ritual: first I was the inner spoon, then it was his turn.

I was thinking about what a therapist had suggested nearly a year before. She inspired me to create my Mom Box, but that hadn't been her only grand idea. *Why don't you visit your brother?* she had asked. *You have the means now.*

At the time, while I acknowledged that my software engineering job would easily fund plane tickets, I didn't want to stomach the stress of a reunion. I adored Aaron but hadn't seen him in a decade. We'd barely spoken since he'd left home. Though excited by the prospect of seeing him and meeting my two nieces, I worried he might not want to see me. He chose to leave, perhaps so hurt by our childhood that he preferred to never look back. Or maybe I had meant less to him than he had meant to me. Maybe I was just some kid, holding onto feelings for a brother who had forgotten I existed. Meanwhile, the seed she planted germinated in the background of my life.

Lulled by the faint highway traffic sounds just beyond the walls of Bob's ancient apartment building, I remembered the countless afternoons spent on monkey bars or in Aaron's bedroom, listening to his wild stories. Even though he was objectively cooler, he liked the real me—just as Mom had. This was at a time when the popular girls at school regularly crinkled their eyebrows at me. I didn't know what the *Banana Republic* on their matching t-shirts meant. I wasn't making out with boys like they were. I got too excited about answering the teacher's questions in class. But with Aaron, I didn't have to worry about fitting in.

As I lay awake in Bob's bed that night feeling more at peace than I had in years, the seed seemed to have grown into a sapling, captivating with its dewy chartreuse leaves sparkling. While I was still afraid to find out that Aaron wanted nothing to do with me, I also recognized the unlikeliness of that outcome. I pictured a tidy future of gradually increasing connection. The visit would be followed by frequent, easy phone conversations, then lengthy, laughter-filled holiday visits: like a family Christmas movie. It would culminate in the kind of intimate sibling relationship I read about in novels, the kind we had had when we were little kids, but without the bullying.

That night, a sense of urgency washed through my body, preventing sleep. I acknowledged that if I waited too long, I might never see him again. Tomorrow was never guaranteed, as I had learned so long ago.

"I think I want to go see my brother."

I felt Bob roll over to face me. "Yeah?"

"Yeah." I paused, gathering courage. "Would you come with me?"

"Of course."

I smiled in the dark, leaned in, and kissed his mouth. "Thanks." I rolled over, and we cycled through our spooning routine once more before falling asleep.

The next afternoon, after eating gyros with Bob in a loud cafe and driving back to my place, my stomach tumbled over itself with nerves. I wanted to watch TV, eat ice cream, or reorganize a drawer: anything to distract me from the feelings. Instead, I sat in the dining chair that I kept in front of my desktop computer in the corner of the living room, a makeshift office in my one-bedroom suite. I would force myself to contact Aaron before I'd let myself do anything else. From the social networking website that had recently become popular, still called The Facebook then, I sent him a message asking if Bob and I could fly out to visit.

After hitting Send, my mind wandered into the future. Would our conversations be as easy as the ones in his childhood bedroom, boombox beats in the background? Or as halting as the occasional and out-of-the-blue calls he'd made in his first years away, when he complained that I *didn't really have anything to say*? It had been almost eleven years. Would he even be the Aaron I remembered, or had he grown into a completely different person?

To my surprise, my tech-averse brother replied within a single day: *It would be so great for you guys to come!*

Several months later, my heart raced as I directed Bob through the sparse streets of Seaford, Delaware, with a printout from MapQuest: "Turn right. Keep going. Turn left at that light."

Bob and I had flown into Baltimore the day before, where we celebrated Halloween in the old city with a haunted walking tour and seafood. Early that morning, we picked up our rental car and drove two hours southeast through mostly remote areas. We passed fields of dormant yellow grass dotted with trees barely hanging onto their red and orange leaves. We passed chicken coops and Royal Farms gas stations. Now, we were finally moments from our smalltown destination.

When we turned onto his street, I saw Aaron standing with a woman in a driveway. He wore jeans and an open brown bomber jacket, his face partially concealed by wrap-around mirrored shades. Even in sunglasses, even after more than a decade, I knew him instantly.

"Are you sure?" Bob asked.

"Yeah. That's my brother."

Bob parked in front of the patchy yard. Hands shaking, I flung open the car door, leapt out, and jogged up the short gravel drive. I watched Aaron quickly wipe at unwelcome tears with his wrist. Before either of us could speak, I wrapped my arms around him, squeezing my right cheek against his shoulder. Teardrops cascaded down my chilly cheeks.

This was the hug I'd been yearning for for years.

I adjusted my arms from their awkward initial landing position and took a breath, relaxing. I expected to smell the Drakkar Noir he wore throughout high school, but instead it was the biting scent of men's deodorant. I locked my fingers around my wrists behind him and kept my right ear pressed to his body, my tears collecting on his sweatshirt and jacket. I felt velcroed to him, like the putting together was effortless but the taking apart would require force. I didn't want to ever let go.

Eventually, we loosened our hug enough to make eye contact. We took in each other's faces, which made us both smile wider, cry more, and go straight back into our vice-grip embrace. I was surprised by our relative heights: he was only a few inches taller than me. Also, he looked so much happier than I expected. When we finally stepped out of our embrace, my whole body shivered with a spontaneous release of tension. I hadn't been sure this day would ever come.

Aaron, apparently thinking the same thing, said, "I thought I'd never see you again, kid."

Kid. No one had called me *kid* since... Suddenly I was a pre-teen again, sitting on the edge of his waterbed, eagerly awaiting whatever my big brother might say next. The four of us made our way inside as his girlfriend and I laughed at how Aaron had tried to hide his tears behind his orange sunglasses. I already liked her.

Once inside, we were introduced to four energetic children: her boys and his girls. Aaron was eager to begin our tour, and I obliged, longing for his presence even while experiencing it.

When Aaron had told me they lived in a double-wide trailer, I pictured something dingy and cramped. Instead, I found myself in a thoughtfully-decorated open kitchen and living area. The house was painted in warm tones with bright white trim. Pendant lights hung above the bar-height kitchen counter.

"I bought this thing real cheap," he said. "Everyone told me it was a stupid idea. I mean, covered in mold, floor to ceiling like you wouldn't believe. I had to gut the whole thing. Borrowed a sandblaster to get the mold out."

I thought about the small two-story house where we grew up. Our parents bought it for next-to-nothing after marrying at nineteen. Dad had a knack for household projects. He could troubleshoot a plumbing leak long before YouTube; he could turn planks of treated wood into a sprawling deck as expertly as his carpenter father. Mom was a frugal and fearless do-it-yourselfer with her own red toolbox. Together, they spent years meticulously repairing and remodeling that little house. They painted rooms, converted a garage into a den, and added a second-floor deck. By the time I was born, the only trace left of its dilapidated origins was the mention of vulgar drawings hidden behind drywall. Like father, like son.

As Aaron grinned at me, lifting and dropping a toilet lid to show off the special hinges designed to prevent loud slams, I let part of my awareness shift to other matters—I hoped undetectably so.

He was thin; was he too thin? He didn't behave like someone actively using drugs, but I knew he'd tried some of the worst. I noticed the sores that spotted his sunken cheeks. While I followed him into the hall, my mind played a game of two-person toss, a ball soaring from *teenage acne scars* on one side to *meth addict sores* on the other. Acne; meth. Which was it? Could former meth addicts still have marks? None of the internet articles I'd read during one of my worry fits had covered *former* meth addicts.

After the tour, we all sat together in the living room. Aaron and Leigh-Anne made a surprising pair. She had milky smooth skin and a large frame. He maintained a quiet presence while she carried the conversation forward with bubbly chitchat. I listened as best as I could while stealing glances across the room to see the kids at play. I was so excited to see myself in his girls, from my older niece's freckled face to my younger niece's endearing habit of putting away her toys on the right shelves, reminiscent of my lifelong affinity for well-organized spaces.

While Leigh-Anne continued to catch me up on the lives of their children, extended family, and exes, I watched Aaron stand up. He caught the eldest kids on the verge of an explosion.

"Hey," he said firmly but with patience. "What did we just talk about yesterday? Don't make fun of your sister."

He took Leigh-Anne's ancient dog outside, then swung into the kitchen to refill someone's drink. I saw Aaron as I never had before, excelling in the roles of father and partner.

Later that night, Bob and I laid knotted up together in our dreary motel room, a comforter crisp beneath us. I sobbed into his t-shirt. I was impressed by my brother's home and his family life. At the same time, the few teeth he had left were black and rotted. He moved around constantly and said he slept only a few hours a night. I couldn't stop agonizing over whether the rehab program he was in years before had cured his addictions. How could I find out? Would I ever be alone with him? What would I even say? *Hey, you kinda look like shit. Are you on drugs? You should quit.* What did I know about narcotics and addiction, anyway?

We spent the next day playing games with the kids. In the evening, I accompanied Aaron to the grocery store. He stopped me in the entryway.

"See that?" he asked, looking slightly up.

"What?"

"There," he pointed to the fluorescents lining the ceiling. "The lights. See how the first ones are hung in a nice, even row, and then they start getting all sloppy?"

"Yeah." It was obvious, the latter lights veering off-course some six inches left or right of the light fixture before it.

"That's where I quit, and some other guy took over. That's what I was telling you. I like things to be *perfect*. These other guys, they just don't give a damn."

We talked the whole time he shopped. He told me about the engagement ring he had already bought Leigh-Anne, and about the rising lot rent in his neighborhood. There were brief seconds where I lost track of reality, as if no time had passed since the countless afternoons we spent in his bedroom talking about the events of our very different school days. We were alone, but I couldn't ask him about his drug use. Why bring him down and ruin this mesmerizing moment?

Back at the house, Aaron cooked scrapple, a greasy loaf made of pork trimmings and flour, and the trailer filled with savory scents. When Bob asked, "What's scrapple?" Aaron laughed.

"The name says it all: *scrap-ple*. It's the scraps most people won't eat. They only sell it in, like, Delaware and Maryland. It's grown on me."

He had an accent. I hung onto the way he curved the word *grown*, as if it rhymed with *down*. I wondered what the transition was like for him. Did he show up in this tiny town and deliberately begin to mimic the people around him? Or did it happen gradually without him noticing?

He and Leigh-Anne fed the children first, filling plates and lining them up on the counter. After corralling the kids up to the bar, they monitored from nearby, expertly deflecting requests for sweets and soft drinks. The whirlwind of activity didn't last long. Soon the kids were happily entertained by booming video games in the boys' room and hair ties in the girls' room, and we adults sat down to eat. Toward the end of our meal, Aaron said he wanted to ask me a question.

"I've never understood," he started. "We had the same parents, grew up in the same house. How did you end up there," he pointed my way, "and I end up here?"

"I don't know." My cheeks suddenly ablaze with shame, I stuttered, "You, uh... had it a lot tougher than me."

It was true. An aunt had told me a story of young Aaron being sent to his room without supper for punishment, Mom later sneaking him a sandwich behind Dad's back. There were stories of beltings that bore no resemblance to the weak butt taps I endured, a claim that explained why I still jumped at the sound of a snapping leather belt.

I was just a child then, lucky to have been born second and female. Yet guilt knocked the wind out of me as I sat in Aaron's kitchen that autumn evening, my feet dangling from the barstool. How could I have moved on with my gilded life and left him to fend for himself? What was wrong with me?

"I've just always wondered, ya know."

"Yeah," was all I could say. *Me too.* I focused on catching my breath while padlocking a lid over the sludge that gurgled inside. I knew then that I'd never be able to ask him about his drug use. I wondered, but not enough to stick my snobby nose into his business.

After dinner, we gathered on the couch for group pictures: a welcome distraction.

"Okay, you two get on the couch first," Leigh-Anne directed Aaron and me with a smile. I fidgeted, uncomfortable with the unbounded being-near-Aaron joy that hadn't let up in three days, the weight of the trip soon ending, and an eagerness to flee all of the emotional intensity. I missed my simpler, predictable life at home.

I shifted my focus to the composition of our photograph, leaving the present to plan how I would hold onto it. We situated ourselves in the center of the plush tan sofa. With my left arm against Aaron's right, I turned my palm up at the same time he reached out. Holding Aaron's hand was unusual. It wasn't the smooth, puzzle-perfect fit of Bob's hand, but it was wonderful. I felt like his little sister again: safe.

"Okay, you two, smile!"

I offered a real smile, brimming with joy and gratitude.

They invited us to stay for breakfast the next morning, but I made up a bogus excuse about travel time. I'd hated goodbyes since I was seven. I just wanted to get it over with; was that too much to ask?

After dark, before I climbed into the rental car and left his circle for the last time that weekend, Aaron and I talked on the curb, lengthening the farewell. He inquired about our dad.

"He's so overweight," I whined, voicing my persistent Dad-worry. "He never exercises, eats whatever he wants. He has ice cream, like, every night!"

Aaron looked at me then in a way that made my insides curl in on themselves. I felt I could fall to my knees if it weren't for the bracing tension coursing through me from neck to feet. It was his I'm-disappointed-in-you look.

"Come on, ice cream? It could be a hell of a lot worse; you know that."

"I know," I responded, eyes down to the ground now, my mind flipping through all the reasons I should be grateful instead of complaining. Dad wasn't battling a drug addiction. He wasn't dead. The man just liked his sundaes. All those years, all of my apparent maturity into adulthood and two college degrees, and Aaron could still school me with his big-brother wisdom.

Finally, reluctantly, we exchanged another hug, and I climbed into the low passenger seat.

Back on the main road, Bob asked, "How ya feeling?"

I sighed a held breath. "Good. I'm glad we came." In spite of all the emotional heaviness of the trip, I was proud to have reclaimed my own solid relationship with Aaron, distinct from the wobbly three-legged scrap left behind after Mom's death. I looked out the side window at the night sky, smiling at the street lights and at the stars I couldn't see.

I had my brother back.

13 NOW

My brother is fine.

I offered an automatic smile to my coworker as I passed, carrying a plated black bean burger back to my cubicle. I'd recently shifted to vegetarianism, and this new-to-me convenience meal had become my favorite lunch. Whether it was the satisfaction of running or the dissatisfaction with my gradual weight gain, something had inspired me to find a more healthful diet. My internet research pointed to the lower cancer risk of plant-based diets, and then shocking documentaries about the food industry pulled on my animal-lover heart strings. I was experimenting with a new identity, cooking foods my family never ate, and enjoying the process. Plus, I was losing excess weight.

I was energized to work through lunch, squeezing a week's worth of tasks into three days. Thursday would be the July fourth holiday. Bob and I had fun plans to stay overnight in a nearby town where I was going to run my first race.

When I reached my cube, my cell phone was vibrating on my desk. Leigh-Anne was calling. Though we emailed occasionally, my sister-in-law rarely called, and never mid-workday. My heart sped up. My breath caught in my throat. Scenarios flitted through my mind. Maybe Aaron was drinking too much again. Maybe they were having money problems, and she was reaching out in desperation. I set my meal down and attempted to reassure myself.

Chill out. It could be nothing. She could just be checking in.

"Hey, Leigh-Anne! I don't usually hear from you in the middle of the day." I added, faux-joking, "Should I be worried?"

A brief pause. "I have some bad news." Leigh-Anne's voice was flat and emotionless.

"Okay," I said, my stomach suddenly so tense I was barely breathing. I walked toward the privacy of a conference room and reminded myself to inhale. *Something happened to her*, I told myself, *not Aaron*. Maybe it was her parents, or her sister who I met once. She needed me to be calm. I would be calm.

Be calm.

"What's going on?"

"Aaron was in an accident this morning, and he was killed."

I hadn't made it far from my desk. My legs stopped moving. I was frozen in the aisle, between an unoccupied cubicle and the beige five-foot wall of another. With my left elbow posed in a bend, my hand a mechanical extension cradling cell phone to ear, I replied, "What?"

Leigh-Anne repeated in monotone, "Aaron was in an accident this morning. He passed away."

"Wh-, what kind of accident?"

"It was a motorcycle accident. He was hit by a truck."

I didn't understand. Her words didn't make any sense. "Is he at the hospital?"

"No."

"Where is he?"

When she responded, "He's at the morgue," there was an exhale of weary compassion in her voice.

The *morgue*? I fell into a cross-legged position, sobbing on the floor with my forehead in my empty palm. My brain switched frantically between reality and make-believe:

Dad and I will just fly out and go see him in the hospital. He'll get better.

No: he's a motionless corpse lying on a cold metal stretcher in a morgue, and I have to break the news to Dad.

No. No, not that. He'll be back at work welding again in no time, as soon as he recovers.

"I'll call you back later," I cried, and as she answered "okay," I was already hanging up. Electricity pulsed down my arms with an uncontrollable yearning, a rare earth magnet approaching one of its kind: I wanted to be held. I stood, took some tissues from a coworker's vacant desk, and speed-walked to the front lobby to tell our maternal receptionist.

"Diana?" I screeched, my arms opening.

"Oh, no, sweetie." She stood and reciprocated a quick embrace, then stepped back. My shoulders tightened in frustration. Her touch hadn't made any of the hurt go away. "What happened? Are you okay?"

I answered concisely, "My brother died," so I could focus on rethinking my hug strategy. I was too scrambled to get anywhere, though: everything was moving so fast.

"How?"

"A motorcycle accident."

After a pause, she asked, "Recently?" her face wrinkled in confusion.

I nodded. "This morning. I just found out." I felt pissed that I had to resolve *her* confusion. I wished she would just *shut up* and feel sorry for me, without me having to say anything. I felt like someone the morning after their first *Fight Club*: beaten to shit in places no one could see. But wasn't it painted on my face?

Being lunchtime, I was quickly surrounded by coworkers. As I filled them in, Diana accompanied my story with grave looks, her eye contact held a beat longer than the generally accepted norm, as if psychically commanding the room. My shoulders were no longer tense with resentment. Either those subsequent rounds of explanation moved more smoothly with two of us to tell the story, or I was much less there.

They were all saying versions of, "Oh, Mandy, I'm so, so sorry," their eyebrows bent with concern. A work friend, a soft-spoken mom who'd been mistakenly called *grandma* by another dance recital parent, hugged me into her warm bosom. She squeezed tight and let me stay. Eventually, I took a full breath. It felt like my first in years.

Dan appeared with open arms and a pained face. Against his soft torso I smelled deodorant, and he became ordinary, unscary. Others hugged me, mostly robotically, one after another: a wedding receiving line gone wrong.

Mark appeared and then promptly disappeared for a bit. He returned and held out my cell phone, letting me know he'd called Bob. If I hadn't already been crying, I would have cried with gratitude.

I started to think about my next steps, aware of my responsibility from the moment I had hung up with Leigh-Anne. Though our two families were cordial, as far as I knew, Leigh-Anne didn't talk to anyone else from Aaron's past. My dad called relatives only by virtue of Cheri's urgings, and she had had no incentive to encourage this relationship. Cheri and Aaron never got along.

I said, "I have to go tell my dad." Had I already said that?

I explained that he worked just across town, and that I wanted to tell him in person.

"You shouldn't be driving," someone said. "One of us can take you."

I shouldn't be driving?

I was being looked at, being asked to pick a driver. The simple decision felt like a calculus equation from *A Beautiful Mind*. I wanted a silent commute. Or did I want to talk? And what if I changed my mind mid-route? How far away was Dad's work, again? Wait, what was I deciding?

"Frannie," I eventually announced. My work friend was sensitive enough to listen, and not so sensitive that she'd need the comfort of conversation. Someone handed my phone back to me.

My purse hung from my shoulder, though I didn't remember getting it from the drawer under my desk. That phrase, *drawer under my desk*, felt recent, though. Had I spoken it? I walked with Frannie through the front doors, to the blindingly sunny parking lot and her black SUV.

During the fifteen-minute drive, I hovered above acceptance. I was focused on the task at hand. In my head, I rehearsed what to say to Dad. What I wanted was a long hug, held against his solid chest. I wanted us to cry together, to take time to be with this new truth together. I shoved that hope down into my gut. I couldn't afford to be unrealistic.

As we neared the dealership, I blew my nose, dried my cheeks, and took some deep breaths. Frannie dropped me off just outside the service entrance. I planned to stick with my dad and deal with picking up my car later. I stepped out of the front seat and thanked her, hoping she'd drive away as soon as I shut the door. I didn't turn around to check.

I walked from the lot into the wide covered drive that ran through the middle of the dealership, separating the sales area and its suited men from the service garage. Realizing that I wouldn't be able to get the words out to say who I was there to see, I turned to avoid the service desk. I didn't know if they recognized me as Mike's daughter, or if they noticed the shocked grief on my face. The whole space was a blur. I was hyper-focused on obeying the persistent voice in my head (*You've got a job to do*) and predicting how the next few minutes might unfold.

I headed to my dad's stall in the back of the massive garage, the clacking of my flats against the concrete echoing loudly. My legs moved as if with their own sense of purpose, in opposition to my need for comfort. The motor-oil smell in the air offered a slight calm. It was how my dad came home smelling every workday of my youth. Now, he stood in his work uniform, a gray jumpsuit spotted with grease, beside a car hoisted up in the air to eye level. He noticed me well before I got to him. He gradually stopped his twisting of a tool and stepped forward, gripping a rag stained dark and looking at me. I had never shown up to his workplace unannounced.

In his stall, I returned his eye contact, took a breath, and started. "Dad, I have some bad news."

"Okay."

"Leigh-Anne called."

He replied matter-of-factly, "Aaron killed himself."

That guess being so close to the surface sent chills down my spine. I'd been bracing myself for news of Aaron's death since he left us fifteen years earlier. It never occurred to me that Dad might be doing the same. I knew he desperately wanted to be wrong, and I was grateful to be able to give him that much. But what I had to say wasn't exactly better.

"No, Dad, he was in a"—the tears began again—"motorcycle accident this morning, and he died." I stood in his stall quietly crying. He remained straight-faced and immediately busied himself, turning away from me to tighten something on the hoisted car.

"What are you doing?" I asked.

"Well, I gotta get this car ready for my buddy to take over. I'm probably not gonna be here tomorrow, so…" He walked over to the royal blue Rusty Wallace toolbox at the back of his stall, opened a drawer, and put away the tool that had been in his hand. Then he called out to his boss. Motioned him over to his stall.

The only man in sight wearing a clean white button-up walked diagonally across the floor toward us. Once within earshot, he called out cheerfully, "Hey, Mike! What's going on?" His smile faded when he saw my face.

"Well," Dad started, in an eerily sing-songy voice, "I guess my son just died, so uh, I'm gonna need to take some time off."

His manager crinkled his eyebrows. He looked from my dad to me and back again.

"I'm gonna hand this truck over to Tim," Dad continued. "I'll let him know where it's at and everything. The lady's gonna be in tomorrow and there's a belt we need to replace…"

"Mike," he interrupted. "Don't worry about that. Take whatever time you need."

"I don't know when I'll be back. I mean, he lives in Delaware and, I mean he…"

"Mike, don't worry about it. Go. Leave. Be with your family."

Dad continued to tinker in his stall while I walked to the open end of the garage to call Cheri. I told her the same way I told Dad.

"Oh my God, his poor kids!" she lamented. She sounded shocked and was talkative. She asked me questions about his daughters' current custody status and speculated about the drama that might follow. I fidgeted with my eyes, looking at the concrete under my shoes and outside to the lot of vehicles, the sun reflecting off windshields and tailgates. I ignored what questions I could and answered the rest briefly. I was exhausted. I wanted to collapse like a rag doll and suck my thumb. When I hung up, Dad was nearby.

"Where's your car?" he asked.

"It's at work. Can I just go to your house with you?" *Daddy* remained on the tip of my tongue. I climbed into the familiar front seat of his pickup and let him take control.

Bob was on the doorstep of my parents' four-bedroom ranch not long after we arrived, out of breath as if he had just finished a sprint rather than an air-conditioned Interstate commute. We sat shell-shocked on their awkwardly deep burgundy couches. I wanted to curl up in Bob's lap, to be showered in his affections, and yet I didn't. Bob and I weren't big on PDA around my parents, who I rarely saw kiss and had never seen hold hands. Even on that tragic afternoon, Dad and Cheri lacked any apparent desire for closeness. They sat across the wide room from each other while I struck a balance by nestling up against my husband's side.

Each of us looked down at a cell phone, searching for additional articles. I re-read the one we'd found over and over, hoping to glean new insight from its limited details.

The accident occurred around 7:10 a.m. Was this Aaron's typical Monday morning routine, I wondered, or was the motorcycle a fun change of pace? Had he been running late, scheduled to be in by seven? *The truck subsequently turned into the path of the motorcycle.* But why? And then there was the worst of all missing details, the one I couldn't shake from my awareness but didn't want to know, either. *He was pronounced dead at the scene.* But when *exactly* did he die? Immediately on contact, or...

"Mike, you should call your sister." Cheri's voice snapped me back to my spot on the living room couch. We went through the list of relatives and decided who would call who. Dad would call most everyone: his sister and brother, their adult kids, Cheri's relatives. I offered to call Mom's family. I listened just long enough to hear that Dad's calls were as unusual and matter-of-fact as his exchange with his boss. Then I walked into Dad and Cheri's bedroom, closed the door, and sat on the side of their bed, a box of Kleenex within reach. I let myself make the easiest call first. Married into our family, my warm and candid Aunt Mary Pat was the oddball who not only tolerated but seemed to enjoy emotionally complex conversations.

"Hey, Mary Pat. It's Mandy."

"Hi! How are you?"

"I'm okay." What was the right amount of small talk for a call like this? "I'm actually calling with some bad news." I collected myself, feeling grateful for her silence. "Aaron was in a motorcycle accident this morning, and he died."

I heard a gasp. "I'm so sorry! Wow... How are you and your dad doing?"

"Not great," I answered. "But we're together. I'm at his house now."

"That's good. Oh, Mandy... You know Tom and I got to spend some time with him when he came to Omaha for his honeymoon. What was that, four years ago?"

"Yeah. And grandma's funeral."

"That's right, he was here for that."

Now I was providing the silence while I waited for her to process what had happened to her young nephew. Her energy felt big, like it took up space all around her. I imagined her pacing through her cozy living room, passing in front of the plentiful furniture that accommodated her family of seven.

"I'm so sorry to hear this. Aaron—" She took a breath. "We all loved Aaron so much. Do you think you'll fly out there for the funeral?"

"Probably." One thing at a time.

"Good. That's nice. Thank you for calling, Mandy. I love you. And I'll be praying for you and your Dad, and for Leigh-Anne and his kids."

"Thanks, Mary Pat. I love you, too."

"Okay, bye, sweetie."

"See ya." *And thank you for keeping our call short*, I thought.

I greeted Aunt Patty with the same rehearsed lines. Unsurprisingly, she was shocked. But where my other aunt seemed to get bigger, Patty seemed to shrink. I thought I could hear her crying, but it was soft. Even if she had been standing when she answered my call, she was probably sitting now, bent over herself, wishing she had a tissue. Or maybe she pulled a crumpled one from the pocket of her off-brand high-waisted jeans. The same style Mom would be wearing, if she were alive. Our conversation flowed quite similarly, but at a lower volume. She'd be praying for our family, too. When I hung up, there was a new tension in my chest. I hated that that was the first time I'd talked to Patty in years.

Once all of the important calls were completed, my parents debated where to go to dinner.

"Let's go to that seafood place downtown," Dad offered.

"Ugh, gross," Cheri spat, her forehead crinkled. "You know I don't like fish. That steakhouse, what's it called?"

"You said you'd try it with me," he whined.

It was oddly both surreal, given the evening's traumatic context, and totally mundane to witness them arguing as they always did before such decisions.

"Outback!" Cheri suddenly remembered. "The last time, though, they burnt my steak to a crisp. Remember?"

"Come on, we go there all the time!"

Bob and I waited silently for one of them to win. When they finally settled (somehow both unhappily) on Outback Steakhouse, we quickly agreed in near unison.

"Sounds great!"

"Great!"

We'd exchanged enough knowing glances to have solidified an unspoken plan. Bob announced to my parents, "We'll meet you there."

"Oh," Cheri started, "You don't want to ride with—?"

He interrupted, nodding in faux disappointment, "We would, but, we'll have to get going right after dinner to let Keira out."

Thank God for this man.

The second I shut the passenger door of Bob's Impreza, effectively obscured behind its tinted windows, I crumpled. The familiar hug of the upholstered bucket seat supported me from back to thigh. I squeezed my eyes closed and heard him start the car, felt the blast of AC kiss my face. I squinted my eyes open again to look at my lap, to drag my floating self back down to earth. "I can't believe he's dead."

"I know, baby. I'm so sorry." He reached out his right arm, and I turned my body toward him so I could hug it to my chest.

"I want to go home. I just want to go to bed." Tears fell down my cheeks onto his forearm.

"I know, baby," he repeated with a softness that hit the spot like PMS chocolate: exquisite, yet not nearly enough. "But you need to eat something. It'll be real quick, and then we can go home, and you can go straight to bed."

I sat upright, panting, and wiped away my tears. My stomach growled as if to punctuate his point. I nodded and said, only half-believing, "I can do this."

"You can do this."

The words parroted back in his steady voice solidified my faith. I *could* do this. I'd done it before.

14 THEN

Moms don't die.

My nimble mom hustled around the first floor, tidying after a hectic evening spent babysitting her sister's two young sons. Aaron and I sat cross-legged on the carpet near our Christmas tree. I inhaled the fresh fir scent while admiring the magic of flashing lights: green on a glass angel, a miniature wooden Nativity scene briefly blued, a portrait of Aaron and baby me awash in orange, then the angel green again. At seven years old, I wasn't yet irritated by their hodgepodge aesthetic or weighed down by the memories they triggered—I loved them all.

My body buzzed with excitement for the fun of the season. All of my cousins were in town, their families having made their way in minivans back home to Omaha from Wisconsin and Denver. No snow had stuck to the ground yet that year, but the biting temperatures told me those sparkly white puffs were on their way. With them would come snowmen and snow forts in the front yard, built with friends from down the street. Presents were piled under the tree. I was sure many of them held the toys I'd requested.

Every time Mom stepped out of view, Aaron picked up another box and shook it, or put it to his ear and tipped it slowly, listening. I could only watch in awe. He seemed infinitely brave and smart. His investigation was complex, as Mom had stopped writing our names on the tags. This was due to Aaron's alleged practice of secretly unwrapping and rewrapping his own gifts, a defiance I could hardly imagine. That year, she had labeled our gifts with mysterious numbers.

"We should open one," Aaron said to me once Mom was out of earshot.

"It's not Christmas yet."

"In two days, it is. Plus, look at how many there are. We should get to open *one* tonight."

Beginning to see his logic, I exclaimed, "Yeah!"

"Okay, go ask Mom."

I knew to pay close attention when Aaron told me to do something. One time he begged me to try his *really good beef jerky*, and only once it was on my tongue did he admit it was precisely what I had suspected: a dog treat.

This idea seemed like a great one, as they all did at first. I *really* wanted to open a present. I jumped up and ran into the kitchen.

"Mommy, can we open a present?"

"Honey, it's not Christmas yet."

"It's close!"

She opened the dishwasher, piling gold butterfly-rimmed dinner plates onto her forearms. A seemingly healthy and joyful thirty-five-year-old, my mom was petite at five foot six and barely more than one hundred pounds. While her voice had the gentle lilt of an attentive mother, her hands were rough with household labor.

She hadn't answered me.

"Just one?" I pleaded.

She looked up at me then and smiled, apparently on the verge of caving in. Excited, my mind raced to decide which present I'd pick: *The biggest one. No, the heaviest one!*

Before she could respond, my dad stepped into the kitchen, capturing her attention. With a quick squeeze of my mom's behind, he set his empty glass on the counter and suggested, "Why don't you kids help your mom out for a change, then maybe we'll think about a present?"

"How 'bout we do the dishes," Aaron offered, "then we each get to open one?"

I stomped my feet. "I don't wanna do the dishes!"

"You could fold the towels?" Mom added while pouring Dad's refill.

"But *Mahm*!"

"Forget it," Dad said, announcing the end of the debate. "The answer's No." Mom handed him his drink, and he returned to the den. I crossed my arms over my chest and turned toward Mom so that Aaron wouldn't see the tears I felt coming. I didn't like being called a crybaby.

She leaned close. "Why don't you go pick out a book, and I'll be there in a minute, okay?"

I nodded. She always made me feel better.

Once, after catching me with my nose in the purple and white lilac bushes that poked through our backyard fence, she brought out her kitchen shears and cut stems for me, gifting me with their captivating scent. When I expressed grief after my great-grandma died, she encouraged me to journal. I sat on her bathroom counter while she listened to me read back what I had written about Great-Grandma Rerucha's crispy Bohemian rosette cookies and fluffy powdered-sugar-dusted kolaches, the things I loved most about our annual visits to her farmhouse in rural Butler County, Nebraska. And when my beloved yellow Labrador retriever broke a hip and had to be put down, she assured me it was okay to cry.

Like then, my tears evaporated. Already mentally flipping through my extensive *Berenstain Bears* collection, I headed to my room, the presents momentarily forgotten.

Soon, Mom was sitting in my bed beside me, and I was snuggled into her right side, the comforter over both of our bottom halves. I listened to her read *Get in a Fight*. It was one of my favorites. As she flipped through each page, she adjusted her voice to play each character in the friendly bear family: Mama Bear, Papa Bear, Sister, and Brother. They were a family of four like us.

"Look," I exclaimed, pointing at the illustration, "Sister has a lunch box." I'd seen the picture countless times before, but I liked to stretch out reading time as long as possible.

"She does," Mom agreed.

"And there's a bluebird."

"Yep."

"And a squirrel!"

"Okay," she said, meeting my grin with hers and turning the page beneath my hand, "let's see what happens next."

When Brother and Sister had made up, Mom closed the book and sang me our nighttime song before kissing me goodnight.

The next morning, I awoke to a voice that was as tender as my mother's but wasn't.

"Mandy, dear, wake up."

I opened my eyes to a face that wasn't quite right. Warm, light eyes like Mom's studied me, framed by similarly permed and feathered hair. As the world came into focus, I realized it was my mom's sister who crouched beside my bed with one hand on my shoulder. Aunt Patty had never woken me up before.

"Where's Mommy?"

"We're gonna go see her."

"Where'd she go?"

"Well... She had a headache, so your dad took her to the hospital."

She glanced toward the doorway then, where Grandma stood, silent. Looking back at me, Patty added with a smile, "Come on, let's get you dressed."

"Okay."

Wait. I was confused. Mom never went to the hospital because of a little headache. "How come she's at the hospital?"

"Well..." she said, thinking for a beat. "The doctors are helping her feel better."

"Where's Aaron?"

"He's at the hospital with your dad."

It seemed strange that he was already there when the day was just beginning for me. But more importantly, everybody was somewhere else together, and I didn't want to be left out. Assuming Mom would be home later that afternoon and opening presents with us at Grandma's that night, our Christmas Eve tradition, I climbed out of bed and got dressed.

I rode along in the backseat of Grandma's car to a parking lot outside of a towering building. Once inside, we rode an elevator up. It was as quiet as church, and I wondered if I was allowed to talk. I looked around but didn't see the sick people I expected. Eventually, we stopped at a long room full of couches and chairs where I saw my family.

"Grandpa!"

My mother's father was a tall and friendly old man whose lap I often occupied. One of the earliest computer engineers, he kept himself well-informed of my grades and rewarded high marks with plush animals that delighted me.

"Hey, there!" He pushed out from the table where he sat so we could hug. "Want to help me with this puzzle, kiddo?"

"Yeah!" I climbed into the chair across from him and looked out over the partially-assembled landscape.

"Can we go see Mommy?"

"Not yet. Your uncle Tom's with her."

"Why?"

Grandpa continued to examine his piles. I was mesmerized by the way he could pick up two identically-green pieces and know they would fit together.

"Grandpa, how come we can't go now?"

"That's just how it works."

Eventually, a nurse stopped outside the waiting room.

"Mr. Partusch?" I knew she meant my father.

Aaron and I followed the two of them down a hall to a tiny room where we all crammed inside. The nurse sat in front of me, leaning in close and describing what we would soon see. I wondered why we had to sit and listen to this woman I had just met instead of going to see Mom.

"Does that make sense?" the nurse asked, looking in my eyes and awaiting an answer.

To be polite, I nodded my head, but I was perplexed. When she explained that my mom was laying on an *egg crate mattress*, I pictured the red plastic crates that held tomatoes in my babysitter's backyard. I wondered why they would make her lay on something so hard. Wasn't it painful? When she said Mom was *restless*, I puzzled over what those two words meant when put together. Probably that she was very nearly asleep: ready for a rest because she hadn't had one.

When the nurse concluded, we followed her down a series of halls until finally arriving at our destination. Inside the large room, I saw someone lying on her back in a narrow hospital bed, people in scrubs standing around her. She moved nonstop: turning her head side to side, kicking her feet under the covers, pushing at the staff with her arms as if wanting to get out of bed. I had never seen my mom from that odd angle in which not even the full profile of her face was visible. She made strange and unsettling whimpering noises.

The fearless nurse walked right up to the bed and said, "LuAnne, your children are here to see you."

Mom didn't look at us. She moaned louder, and I wondered why she wasn't using her words.

"LuAnne!" the nurse repeated in a cheerful, sing-songy voice unlike the one she had used with us. "Mandy and Aaron are here. They're your children, remember? They came to visit you. See?"

The nurse stretched her left arm out toward us, inviting Mom to look, but she was disinterested. She looked back up at the ceiling and continued squirming in the bed. The nurse made eye contact with Dad and subtly shook her head.

"Let's go," Dad commanded.

Not much more was said that day. The doctors were still diagnosing the situation, and my family was hardly able to explain to a child what they didn't understand themselves. Mom spent the evening in the hospital, as well as the next night.

Meanwhile, we carried on with our holiday traditions as best as we could. I got to play with my cousins at Grandma and Grandpa's house. Back home, Dad, Aaron, and I opened our gifts under the tree. Together they cracked the numeric code after we'd opened a few boxes: odd numbers for Aaron, like on his Erector Set, and even numbers for me, like on the swimsuits for my Barbies. I wasn't sure what *odd* and *even* numbers were, and I didn't give it much thought. I had enough on my mind with the unfamiliar mix of emotions stewing in my stomach. The pile of new toys delighted me, even as I was crushed that Mom wasn't there to enjoy watching us open our presents like usual. And unspoken adult thoughts were thick in the air since that morning when Patty had awoken me.

When the only gifts left were the ones for Mom, Dad told us to leave them there, under the tree. He said, "We'll wait until we can open them as a family."

Within a couple of days of my first visit, I went with Dad and Aaron to the hospital to see Mom a second time. By this point, Dad had explained to me that she had had an aneurysm. I understood that a vein in her brain had broken, so she had blood inside of her head where it wasn't supposed to go. It was making her confused to the point where she might not recognize me, I had been warned. Now, in the cab of his pickup truck, Dad explained that the doctor had told Mom about her aneurysm because it wasn't safe for her to keep moving so much.

"What did he say?" I asked, eager for another chance to digest the complicated explanation of her sudden illness.

"He just told her, 'LuAnne, if you don't wanna die, you can't be moving around like that.'" Dad chuckled. "Now *that* she understood."

His blunt words bounced around my second-grade brain, searching for their logical home. But like beat-up books stacked at the library entrance labeled *free*, they didn't have one.

Many years later, Dad would boast that as soon as Mom fell ill, he called his psychiatrist friend for advice on what to tell me and my brother. His friend told him to be honest, so he was. For my dad, this undecorated honesty, which was inseverable from his crude sense of humor, was how you best loved a child in pain.

He continued seriously. "She's on her right side, so she can look out the window. So when we come in, you gotta be real quiet and get to that other side of the room fast. Cuz she's gonna want to look at us, but she can't move her head. You understand?"

"Yeah." *Be quiet and be fast, or else she'll die.*

When we arrived at Mom's new hospital room, Aaron was ahead of me. Before he followed Dad through the doorway, he turned around and put his pointer finger to his mouth.

"I know!" I whispered.

He widened his eyes and straightened his finger to his mouth again. I rolled my eyes but wondered, *Could I whisper?*

Mom was alone and under covers on another narrow bed, this time motionless with her head facing the window, just as Dad had described. I walked delicately after Dad and Aaron, terrified of making a sound. I had brought my favorite Christmas present with me: a Crimp 'n Curl Cabbage Patch Kid with blue eyes and brown hair, just like mine. She came with a comb, a curling iron, and a crimper that shaped her stiff, yarn-sized strands.

"Mandy brought something to show you," Dad told her after our stiff hellos. Then, looking at me, he added, "Go ahead."

I handed my doll up to her.

She exclaimed, "It's beautiful!"

My body tensed. She didn't sound like herself. There was something different about the way she spoke to me, a distance that had never been there before. Plus, this doll was equally as beautiful as the other Cabbage Patch dolls I had at home. And she had seen this one before, first when I thrust the ad in front of her and enthusiastically pointed to its picture, and again when she bought it, wrapped it, and placed it under the tree. Hadn't she?

"Who gave it to you?" she asked.

I looked up at Aaron, then at Dad, but they didn't say anything. I wondered if I was supposed to lie to be nice but assumed it was more right to tell the truth, since Dad was hoping the toy would spark her memory.

"Um..." I swallowed, "you did."

"No," she said with a playful smile, "I couldn't have bought you a doll *this* pretty." She glanced at my dad, then to the doll in her hands, her smile fading. "Hmm."

I wanted to believe that she was joking, but I couldn't. Everything about her, about this conversation, felt off.

"Well," she added, leaving her riddle unresolved, "it's a very nice doll."

She looked at it again, then licked her thumb and began rubbing its cheek. She had noticed the pink and white scuff marking the otherwise pristine plastic face. The motion was not unlike what she had done to address stray food or dirt on my cheek countless times before. When it didn't budge, she licked the doll's cheek and rubbed again.

"Look at that," Dad said in an overly praiseful voice. "So much better." He helped her hand my doll back to me, simultaneously reminding her not to lift her head.

She repeated in the same not-quite-right voice, the kind of slowed-down tone adults sometimes use with children, "That's a very beautiful doll."

While the conversation shifted away from me, I inspected the cleaned-up scuff and scrunched my eyebrows. It looked the same. I stood by her bed while Aaron and Dad talked. I noticed a strange, dirty smell. Dad told me to hold her hand, so I did. I felt the familiar roughness of her skin, her fingers so dry in the winter that she wore latex gloves to put on her pantyhose. There was no comfort in the touch. Physically, all of the boxes for hand holding were checked, yet it was all wrong. I stood perfectly still, petrified of the cords coming out of her and out of the machines near me. I worried, *What if I accidentally get stabbed with a needle and get sick like Mommy?*

As the visit wrapped up, I wandered to the table against the wall to examine her array of gifts: flowers, shiny *Get Well Soon!* balloons, and a stuffed animal. My dad explained that people had sent those presents to my mother, and I wondered who. I thought they should have known that she was too old for a teddy bear, but the other items were well-selected. My favorite was a cute little red felt crab, its black beady eyes peeking up from the dirt of a leafy houseplant.

In the truck on the way home, I asked Dad about the smell in Mom's room. He told me it was urine and explained the concept of bedpans. When I asked why she had to pee in a bucket, he said the doctor didn't want her to get up to go to the bathroom.

Since getting up might make her die, I silently finished for him.

In the days that followed, Dad spent a lot of time in the hospital. Aaron and I usually stayed at home. One night, while we were watching *The Ren & Stimpy Show* in the den, Dad came home excited.

"Wait 'til you guys hear this."

From Dad's updates, I knew that Mom vacillated between awareness and confusion. Since Dad was smiling, I thought with hope, *Maybe she was regular Mommy today?*

"I told your mom I was gonna stop by the store tonight to pick up some mac and cheese for you kids. She's like, 'Don't do that, Mike! There's a ton above the microwave.' I thought for sure she had lost it again, right? Come here, look at this."

Aaron and I followed him into the kitchen, where he opened the cabinet high above the microwave. It was full of blue macaroni and cheese boxes.

"Man, she's real sharp sometimes," Dad added. I liked that kind of story the best.

A couple of days later, he came home and told us Mom was worried they didn't have enough money to cover the month's mortgage payment.

"She said, 'Mike, you can't write that check! It's gonna bounce!'" He grinned.

Aaron stared at Dad, who continued to patiently execute his signature dramatic pause. "And?" my brother prodded.

"That's only happened one time in our whole lives. Once. It was right after we got married, back when we were nineteen."

"So… we're good, you mean? On the bills?"

"Oh yeah, we're fine. I tried to tell her that, but she wouldn't let it go." He shook his head. His smile slowly fell as he continued. "It's like… she's in another time. She even remembered the exact mortgage amount. We paid this house off *years* ago."

I was shocked that Mom believed she was nineteen years old. How scared she must have been to see me and Aaron when, in her world, we hadn't even been born yet.

A week or so into her hospital stay, while the surgeons made plans to repair Mom's aneurysm, my dad prepared us for what might come next.

"If- uh, when your mom comes home, she's not gonna be the same. She's gonna have to learn everything all over again. I mean *everything*: how to talk, how to read. You can help her, can't you, Mandy? Just like she helped you start reading, back when you were in preschool, huh?"

"Yeah. Can I go play now?"

"Yeah. Yeah, go ahead, Punkin."

Alone in my bedroom, I puzzled over my newfound responsibility to teach. I loved how Mom gave me spelling quizzes while she leaned over the bathtub and washed my hair. She taught me multiplication with lined-up pop cans on the kitchen counter, which I hadn't yet learned in school. Maybe I could help Mom like she helped me. I confidently planned how I'd explain things to her. I'd say, *You're not really nineteen, you're a Mommy*. I'd tell her it was okay that she couldn't remember, and she'd see that I was nice. Maybe even part of her brain would know I was her daughter, I hoped. She'd calm down, and I could just talk to nineteen-year-old Mom.

Then, I'd take her to my old preschool with me, where we'd sit side-by-side on the carpet, and I'd help her learn how to talk and to read again. She could paint a little Easter chick like I did, and I'd ask Dad to put it next to mine in the china cabinet beside the fragile plates, vases, and bells that I wasn't allowed to touch. Maybe she'd want to make a paper cat like mine whose eyes changed colors when you spun the wheel behind them. She liked that cat. Then after a while, I told myself, things would be just like they were before. I wouldn't be able to go back to my second-grade class, because they'd be in third or fourth grade by then, but that was okay. Dad said my new job was to take care of Mom, and I was ready.

I went back to school two weeks after Christmas. I knew I had returned later than the rest of my class because when I got there, no one was talking about what Santa brought them. I went straight to my desk and sat low in my seat, barely breathing.

"Good morning, Mandy!" my teacher said. "Now, class, let's welcome back Mandy. Remember how we talked yesterday?" I realized then that she had told the whole class about my mom being sick. My cheeks flushed, and I looked down at my lap so I wouldn't see all of the faces staring back at me.

At recess that week, held inside our classroom given the bitter January cold, I colored alone at my desk. I usually liked playing games or chatting with my classmates but now preferred that no one talked to me.

That Friday, after my short walk home from school, I opened our front door and heard voices. It was my dad's birthday, January tenth, but I knew we weren't having a party. More importantly, I knew that while I was at school, they were going to turn off Mom's breathing machine and see if she could breathe on her own. I hoped she would be able to. I hoped that it was the machine that was making her worse, that her body knew what to do if they would just leave it alone. I headed toward the voices in the kitchen. Passing by the bookshelf in the front room, something on top caught my eye.

I saw the plant with the little red crab from Mom's hospital room, and the direction of the day's events clicked into terrible focus. My whole world dissolved beneath my two tiny feet.

This wasn't supposed to happen.

I was lying on a cushioned lounge chair under the early evening sky, in the lush and private yard of a historic brick house. A warm breeze brushed my skin, and I heard nothing but the rustling of cottonwoods and my own sobbing. Aaron was dead. I held out my arms to Bob, who was standing in wait beside me. He knelt on the grass and hugged tightly.

Bob and I, along with Bob's brother, Mike, and his fiancée, Abby, had rented this house in the small town of Brownville, Nebraska, for the evening. Given my recent loss, they had offered to cancel our overnight adventure, but I insisted we come. I could cry at home, or I could cry there. Plus I wanted the distraction. I was trained up and ready for my first 5K, and I was looking forward to cheering Mike through the finish of his first half marathon.

Beyond Bob's shoulder, Abby looked around the yard as if she wasn't sure what to do, and I didn't mind. I was going to let myself feel the way I felt. A moment later, the tears wrapped up. I felt lighter and settled.

"Can I get you a Kleenex?" Bob asked.

I shook my head. "I want to go inside." He helped me up.

I stuck my head into the screened-in porch and smiled at Mike and Abby, who must have wandered in there during my crying session.

"Don't worry, guys," I said with some sarcasm. "I'm okay. Just had to cry!"

Abby hesitated, then got out, "I can't imagine…"

She seemed self-conscious, and I wanted to tell her, *You're doing it! You're being with me and my grief without trying to fix it. Just allowing it; all of it.* But no; conversation took too much energy.

The next morning, we woke up early so we could be at the starting line well ahead of seven. Bob helped me secure the corners of my paper race number to the front of my tank with the provided safety pins. I was so excited, I couldn't stop smiling. This was the moment I'd been training for: thirty minutes of running on flat pavement, nonstop apart from a few seconds of walking through aid stations to drink water.

At the starting line, I was eager to begin and curious how well I'd do. I was jittery with nerves (hopping left to right, fiddling with my number, asking the group if they thought I had time to pee again), and Aaron hadn't left my awareness. The race official announced the start, and once I passed under the sign, I kicked into my carefully-planned pace. Not a sprint, but not comfortable either.

I was clustered with a lot of other runners at first, but within just a few minutes, I had enough space that I could have stretched out my arms. It was sunny and a bit humid already; I suddenly understood why they start races so early. I trotted along the highway, nestled between grass and dense trees, listening to the satisfying clap-clap of hard rubber soles on concrete. I missed Aaron. *Why did he have to die?* I looked around at the surrounding greenery, searching out animals, hoping to distract myself from my thoughts. It was more beautiful than I had expected: the lush green grass and leafy green trees, a bright blue cloudless sky. Aaron would never get to see grass again, I thought.

"Is this your first time doing Brownville?" A man in a sweat-soaked black shirt jogged beside me, matching my pace and breathing audibly through an open-mouthed smile.

"Yeah," I answered.

"Cool! It's a great course." He wanted me to respond, to join him in breathless conversation, but I wasn't going to divert energy from my running for meaningless chit-chat. "This is my third time, but it's been a few years. Put on a few pounds since then, hah!" He patted his stomach and continued to trot along beside me. "Up ahead there's a little bit of a hill, but then it gets easy again. You're doing great!"

"Thanks!"

"Well, nice meeting you!"

I looked his way and nodded. He dropped back, out of sight. *A hill?* Maybe I should have studied the course map. I wasn't expecting any surprises. I didn't know if I'd be able to keep running if there was a hill. *Mind over matter*, I coached myself. I'd heard racing was more about your mindset than your body. I just needed to keep moving. *You've got this.*

I was part way up the hill before I realized I was on it, as evidenced by the slight extra burning in my quads. The hilliness of my own neighborhood had prepared me more than I'd realized. I nearly maintained my pace throughout the climb and more than made up for any slowing on the downhill. Then the route flattened back out, just as the sweaty man said it would. The runners had thinned so much that I felt almost alone on that long stretch of pavement. With my attention no longer needed to overcome a hill nor maneuver around other athletes, it turned inward. In my chest I noticed the anger that was becoming so familiar. I balled my hands into fists and pumped my arms harder. *Why did Aaron have to die?* It wasn't fair. It was *bullshit* that I'd never get to see him again.

This anger had been coming over me in waves ever since Leigh-Anne's phone call. Sitting alone on our deck or curled up with an afghan on the couch, it stayed with me: tension lodged in my chest and shoulders that I couldn't shake. My mind replayed the same images incessantly, some of which drifted through my mind then. Riding around in Aaron's black Escort trying to rap along with the radio while he leaned way back in the driver's seat, his left hand on the steering wheel and a backward baseball cap high on his head. Sitting on top of the monkey bars when he told me he chewed tobacco; feeling important to be in on his secret. Standing in his Delaware driveway and embracing him after all those years apart. Then, some random man in a pickup that God sent to rip Aaron from my life forever.

Running along the road that day, the thoughts didn't hang on as tight. The anger felt different when I ran. Instead of staying stuck, the tension pulsed throughout my body, down my arms and hands and out, as if dripping from my fingertips. It moved through my torso, down those impressively strong legs, and out of the bottom of my feet, left behind to evaporate on the hot concrete. It felt good.

At the turnaround, I walked for a few seconds while downing a paper cup of cold water from the aid station table. I was afraid my legs wouldn't want to start up again, but they did. We were determined, my body and I, to keep going. To run the best race we could that morning. To make good use of this life with which we were inexplicably gifted.

I picked up my pace a bit for the run back. Looking off toward the spaciousness of sprawling green fields, I imagined Aaron as some kind of angel, in another realm but omnisciently aware of this one. Floating, perhaps, above that gorgeous greenness. He'd think this was cool, me running a race. Doing something I'd never done before. Maybe he'd remind me of the time I gave up on tee-ball, an activity he loved but I never got the hang of, and apologize for calling me a quitter. Tell me with the pure-love wisdom of the afterlife that he knows I'm not a quitter; that I never was.

God, I miss you, Aaron.

Strangers clapped and cheered as I raced under the *Finish* sign a full three minutes sooner than I expected, beaming with pride. I had done it. And I was fast. Bob appeared in front of me, holding out an unlidded plastic water bottle. "Drink this."

"Walk!" I gasped out between shallow breaths and what felt like laughter. "Need. To walk." I guzzled the lukewarm water and walked around in circles hoping to prevent my legs from cramping up, a problem I'd heard other runners complain about. My body was so tired, but strangely, I felt energized. Aaron was still on my mind, yet I felt a new warmth in my chest: joy, peace, even gratitude. Like the unbearable wasn't just bearable: it was *meaningful.* And while I didn't know exactly what it meant, in that moment, I trusted that everything was exactly as it should be.

Less than a week after that horrendous phone call from Leigh-Anne, I flew twelve hundred miles from home with a small group representing all three sides of my family. My cousin Stacey, who was one of Aaron's closest friends growing up, traveled with my parents, Bob, and I. My mom's brother, Tom, would join us the next day.

Waiting in the airport terminal, at the car rental counter, and in the hotel lobby, we spoke with a jittery mix of emotions, light conversation center stage against a dark backdrop. Once we had dropped our bags in our respective rooms, we piled back into the rented SUV and drove to Leigh-Anne's parents' house where everyone was gathered.

We funneled through the ornate front door and stopped inside a large, high-ceilinged living area. When my sister-in-law appeared, my stomach twisted, and I couldn't speak for a moment. I swallowed a few times, trying to absorb the sorrow back into myself. I croaked, "I'm so sorry."

"I know," she said flatly, accepting my hug.

The kids disappeared, and the adults made small talk. I felt confined by the expectation to keep the conversation superficial, so I sat silently near Leigh-Anne in an office and watched her hand-feed single red grapes to her parents' small terrier. I thought I'd remembered reading that grapes were toxic to dogs, but the circumstances tempered my usual need to be right, and I held my tongue. Most of my family stood clumped together in the adjacent living room. Eventually hearing mention of a home tour, I headed that way.

Somewhere deep in that multi-level, many-roomed house, the enthusiasm of the dads forced me to feign interest in floor tiles that were so profoundly and clearly irrelevant, I wondered how anyone was keeping a straight face.

Finally, we headed back outside to our SUV and followed this family we barely knew to the private visitation, just across the state border in Federalsburg, Maryland. American flags hung from light posts lining the sunny main street that led us to a small mortuary, a colonial building of red brick with white wooden columns. Across the street was a flat green cemetery, so small I could make out all four of its edges.

In the expansive entryway of the funeral home, decorated in big floral prints and shiny gold finishes, I lingered. It had been three and a half years since I'd seen my brother. He wasn't supposed to die. I was supposed to see him in just a few months. I took two tissues from a small side table and stepped through the oversized doorway, where I stood, frozen with shock. Off to my right, in the front of the room, was a whisper of Aaron's thin brown hair. The right side of his nose and his hollow cheek were coated in thick makeup, unnaturally bronzed under the lights above a shiny black casket. The realization hit me hard and all at once, a wrecking ball to the gut:

That's my brother.

I squashed whatever was traveling up my throat while warm tears streamed down my cheeks. I turned and sped out of the room, back through the main entrance and into the parking lot so I could cry alone. I fell into a seated position on the concrete, my back against a column, and cradled my forehead in my hands, blocking out the sun. Blocking out everything. *How did he end up there, and I end up here?* Why did he have to die?

Aaron's fifteen-year-old daughter came outside. My sweet freckled niece. Somewhere in my brain there was a fuzzy awareness that she had just lost a parent, not unlike what Little Mandy went through, but the hurting part of my brain had become a bossy security guard, pushing everything but my own needs aside.

She asked, "Are you okay, Aunt Mandy?" with an awkward nurturing tone: a child forced to play adult.

I answered through tears, "I'm okay. I'm just mad." Mad at myself for not being there. Mad that I had left him for so long. She bent down and hugged me, and I instinctively shut down my sobs.

Bob appeared, quiet, and walked around us. He sat to my left, his tan knees bent in khaki shorts and black Chaco sandals on the concrete: an image comforting in its familiarity. I needed more than my soft ladylike crying. Everything hurt.

A moment later, Cheri stepped outside and called my name in a loud, strained voice.

"Pull yourself together and come back inside," she snapped, sounding a touch out of breath. "You have to be strong for your Dad."

Be strong? My jaw clenched with fury. I was so sick of hearing those two words. It was the same shit I was told at my mother's funeral. I watched Cheri walk back inside, the heavy front door closing behind her, before I turned to Bob and spit venom.

"Fuck her! He's my *fucking* brother. She's such a—"

"Hey," Bob interrupted me, a hand on my arm. When I met his eyes, he nodded toward my teenage niece. *Dammit.* He was right. I didn't want to be a bad example, to make her think my hateful reaction was an acceptable one. I took a deep breath.

I took another.

We all headed back inside and lingered in the main mortuary room with Aaron—or rather, with his body—for nearly an hour. I felt exhausted and dazed, the evening passing in a blur. I shifted between feeling compassionately mindful of the kids' needs for hugs or conversation and being a hurt kid myself, scouring the room for Bob, then burying my head in his armpit and crying. When I looked at my brother, there were nanoseconds that I thought he'd open his eyes and say, *What's up, kid?* I didn't want to leave him. After the second or third time that Leigh-Anne's mom gently asked if I might be ready to go, I finally nodded in agreement.

The next morning at the hotel, I read through my notes, refining the speech I'd give that afternoon. My favorite part of any funeral was the storytelling by people who actually knew and loved the deceased. My stomach twisted nervously, but this was important. This was the one thing I could do for him.

I stood in the shower, lathering floral-scented shampoo in my hair and searching my memory for interesting stories to share, when a song came to mind. Suddenly, I was beaming. I had forgotten the tune that Mom used to sing to me before bed:

A bushel and a peck and a hug around the neck. A barrel and a heap and a kiss upon the cheek.

My belly calmed. It wasn't every day I recovered a joyful memory from before.

Back at the mortuary, I stood just inside the main room and mindlessly watched the DVD that looped on a flatscreen TV. A sad churchy melody repeated as images of Aaron faded on and off the screen. Before I left Omaha, I had scanned all of the childhood ones and emailed them to his mother-in-law; most of the others I hadn't seen before then. The first glimpse of each new-to-me photo felt like gulping down water after weeks without: not just quenching but life-giving. The second and third glimpses felt more like a knife twisting in my heart. I didn't know those people he was with, those rooms he was in. We weren't supposed to have been split apart.

After *In Memory* flashed on the screen again, Aaron was a newborn under a colorful afghan. Then, a smiling chubby-cheeked toddler posed in front of a rag doll. He was a little boy in Catholic-school navy pants and a pastel polo, sticking his tongue out at the photographer (Mom?) next to me in a bubblegum pink dress. We were at Grandma and Grandpa's house.

The early teen years were missing, then he was eighteen in brown heavy-duty overalls beside a Christmas tree. I'd always loved that picture. He had his hands stuffed into his pockets and leaned casually to one side. An unreadable smile showcased the lips he thought were too big. He had been living with our grandma then and visiting us to exchange presents. He thanked Dad and Cheri like those overalls were the most perfect gift anyone could have selected for him. I remembered being surprised. I still wonder whether he was faking politeness or thrilled to have received high-quality clothes for a job I didn't know about.

Years later, he was holding my hand on his couch during my first trip to Delaware. He wore a t-shirt Leigh-Anne made him with his favorite comedian's catchphrase (*Git-R-Done!*) in his favorite color (orange). Compared to the preceding teenaged picture, his cheeks had sunken in and his lips were thin lines due to his dental issues. Then he was in a black suit, red vest, and tie posed on the dance floor with his new wife. His hair was slicked back. In the last shot before the title slide, he stood in his living room, decked out in a black and orange riding suit and a black full-face motorcycle helmet. His life in photos ended now, too.

Near the flatscreen, a dozen short rows of folding chairs were arranged perpendicular to the pews, pointing toward the podium rather than the casket. These were reserved for Aaron's family. When the pastor asked us to take our seats for the service, Bob helped shuffle our crew into the rows behind Leigh-Anne and her family in a way that would land me close to my dad. With Cheri on his right side and only one chair to his left, I sacrificed sitting beside my husband so I could be available to my father.

The pastor spoke, and I half-listened, concentrating on being strong. I had to get up and give a speech for my brother. I wouldn't cry. I caught the pastor saying how joyful Aaron must be now. She suggested with a grin, "Maybe he's riding a motorcycle carefree up in Heaven!" I heard a noise to my right and assumed Dad had chuckled at the motorcycle image. I turned, expecting to trade smiles. He was looking down at his lap, sobbing, wiping his nose with a crumpled tissue. Despite his outburst of emotion, Cheri kept her eyes forward and her hands in her lap. Shame over my presumptive smile was quickly overpowered by an acute sadness piercing my heart, making my insides contract: *poor Daddy.* I placed my hand on his broad back and rubbed back and forth. I took yet another deeper-than-normal breath and refocused on keeping my eyes dry.

When the pastor gave me the cue, I stood and walked across the room, careful not to look to my right at the room's focal piece. I stopped behind the podium a few yards from my brother's open casket, allowing myself a glance his way.

Mistake.

I took a breath, blinked my eyes, and gazed unfocused toward the carpet. Finally, I looked at the roomful of his friends and family. I smiled and began to recite fond memories from our childhood. I held out my arms to demonstrate how, as a trusting six- or seven-year-old, I'd be stuck hugging the tree in our front yard after he used his toy handcuffs on me. I pantomimed putting on a backward cap, stretching out my left arm and leaning back slightly, mimicking his early driving style. The room lifted with quiet chuckles. I shared how special it was to visit him a few years back. And at the end, I ventured squarely into cheesiness. If ever there was a time I could get away with cliché, surely my brother's funeral was one?

"As someone who lost a parent at a young age, let me tell you, I *love* to hear people tell stories about my mom. Let's remember the good times we had with Aaron and share those stories, especially with his kids–" I nodded toward his youngest daughter, who was cuddled with Leigh-Anne, "so that his spirit lives on." I took a second to soak in the approving looks from this crowd of strangers, and I walked tall back to my seat. I felt Bob's hand on my shoulder, then his breath against my ear.

"You did great, babe."

Soon, the casket was moved behind a white curtain where immediate family members could say their final goodbyes before it would be closed and transported to the graveside ceremony. When it was Leigh-Anne's turn, I huddled with my family on our side of the room. All day she had been quiet, almost relaxed. Now, she screamed.

"It's not fair! It's not FUCKING FAIR!"

I couldn't hold in my tears any longer. She was right. They were so in love. Both hurt by past partners, they had finally found kindness in each other. And then her soulmate was ripped away from her.

"Hey, don't cry!" Stacey said to me with a crooked grin, intending sarcasm. "Now I'm gonna start crying again."

As a child, I had envied my older cousin's coolness, from her funky late-eighties curls to her bedroom walls. Her parents, unlike mine, let her cover them with taped-up pages torn from fashion magazines. As an adult, I most admired her tell-it-like-it-is tendency. There was nothing I wanted to say then, but it was a comfort to know that I *could* share, and we'd have a real conversation. We stood shoulder-to-shoulder, holding hands. I looked around, pretending not to listen to the explosion happening behind the screen, trying not to absorb Leigh-Anne's agony.

Once we'd all had our last chance to see Aaron, we got in our vehicles and caravanned behind the long black hearse to the chosen cemetery half a mile away. Oddly, it bore the same name as the one in which our mom had been buried: Hillcrest. We gathered in the grass around the casket, now closed and suspended over a hole in the ground. The pastor said a few words. Then, Leigh-Anne's twelve-year-old son stood up and faced the group.

"My dad was a good man," he said, and I felt like I was spying into the future, seeing him as a pastor comforting crowds of grievers. His bravery moved me, my chest warm with admiration.

When the brief ceremony ended, someone handed me an orange rose from the arrangement on top of the casket. Stacey held one, too. Lingering on the cemetery lawn, we stood in separate clusters: his Nebraska family and his Delaware one, further subdividing in ways I could only guess. Was that group of guys work friends? Were those two couples friends, or extended family? Who looked the saddest, and what did they get to know about my brother that I never would? Like groups in a zoo, we were segregated with our kind and curious about those on the other side of the fence. We snuck glances at each other and occasionally ventured into brief interactions.

I kept hearing, "That's his sister." Then one of them would walk over. They'd offer a hand and say with sad eyes, "I'm so sorry for your loss." I didn't understand why they were focused on me. What about our dad? I didn't want the attention. It didn't occur to me that, as the one guest who spoke at the funeral, I may have been the only Nebraskan they felt comfortable approaching.

Back in the rented SUV, I navigated my dad to Aaron's neighborhood so Stacey could see where he had lived. I wished I had visited my brother enough that I didn't need to use GPS. Instead, I kept glancing at the cell screen until the last turn, wishing the houses and trees we passed felt more familiar.

After stopping at the driveway and staring at the mobile home for a moment from behind our tinted windows, we agreed to drive to the crash site.

"It should be just a little bit down this road," I explained once we had exited the subdivision. The air inside the truck felt solid and motionless as we realized how close to home Aaron was when he was killed. Just a few blocks, really. I recognized the road we were looking down from the single photo we had seen on a Delaware news site.

"Yep, this is it," Dad announced.

We slowed down, looking for a broken mailbox or a business parking lot, the few details we knew about the location. I noticed it as we passed.

"Dad, you need to turn around. It's that lot right there."

He joked, "You're gonna make me drive by there again?" My chest warmed at his almost admission of emotion.

Once turned around and back at the small lot next to the crash site, Dad put the gearshift in park. Stacey, Bob, and I got out of the backseat while my parents waited in the front seat. I was surprised they didn't want to get out. I felt pulled to that space around those mailboxes the way I had felt pulled to stand in front of Aaron's casket, desperate to be near whatever Aaron-energy I could find.

We crouched around the curb and examined tiny pieces of plastic and metal that dotted the road, debating whether they were from Aaron's crash. I wasn't sure whether we were genuinely questioning what was in front of us or pretending to disbelieve.

As I looked up from the ground, my gaze met the wooden mailbox post: the last in a row of three, but the only one bare. Its mailbox was almost surely torn off in the accident. I pictured how the accident might have happened: my brother's scrawny body bouncing off of the grill of a white pickup truck, colliding with the flimsy mailbox, and sliding along the grass, maybe into that tree. The otherwise-green lawn was marked with a few deep gashes of brown dirt. I shook the image from my mind and told myself those skid marks were old, from some non-fatal car crash months or years ago. I wanted to know, as if knowing would put me in touch with him again, and I didn't want to know, because to know would be too crushing.

We placed one of our orange roses at the base of the mailbox post. It felt right to see it there. Like we had now honored him in full: from his first breath to his last.

As Dad drove away, Stacey said, "I felt closer to Aaron there than I did at the funeral."

"Yeah, me too," I said. "I'm glad we came."

The crash site had brought me some closure, and in so doing, it opened up space for something more.

Most of our lives, we're unmanned trains charging forward, following our culture's rules without question. We plaster smiles over our frustrations, send rushed email replies as if our lives depended on digital promptness, and stress over dirty dishes left longer than an imagined deadline. Only when a storm knocks us off track do we even realize we were on one. Then we're forced to reevaluate where we are. We're able to consider where we want to go.

"It's a toolbox!" Leigh-Anne's youngest son exclaimed with a smile after tearing away its wrapping paper.

"Mhm." I sat beside him on their deep couch, the rest of the family huddled close, and watched him open its shiny black lid. He paused when he saw the photo of Aaron I'd added to the inside, framed with orange masking tape and accented with father-themed stickers I'd found at a craft store. He put his finger to it before looking back at me with a grin.

"Thanks, Aunt Mandy and Uncle Bob."

Bob and I had returned to Delaware five months after Aaron's funeral to visit Leigh-Anne and the kids. I hoped our presence would offer some sliver of support during their first Christmas season without Aaron. In the weeks leading up to our trip, I had spent hours planning the personalized memorial gifts we brought with us. Now, as we opened them together in their bright living room, I shivered despite the mobile home's comfortable heat, my excited energy uncontainable.

Leigh-Anne's oldest, by then an eternally-annoyed teen, wasn't as impressed as his brother. He read aloud the sticker I'd added. "Dad?" His dad and my brother were not the same man, and he was old enough to value that distinction.

"Be nice," his mother warned.

He formed a polite faux smile and said, "Thank you, Uncle Bob and Aunt Mandy."

"Can I open mine now, Mommy?" their youngest girl asked.

"Why don't you two open together?" I suggested to my nieces. I had messaged with a gal on Etsy to design matching necklaces with an angel wing, an orange topaz charm, and an engraved silver bar: one saying *Dad*, the other *Daddy*.

The oldest gasped. "It says Dad! And look, it's orange! His favorite color!"

"Will you put mine on, Sissy?"

Once the girls' necklaces were on, our focus shifted to the only gift remaining. It was the one I was most excited about. As Leigh-Anne tore off the wrapping paper, I couldn't help but explain, "Aaron made that."

"He did?"

"Yeah, back in high school."

"He never told me about this."

I had long admired the unfinished wooden wall clock that sat for years on a shelf in my parents' basement, gathering dust. Aaron had made it in shop class and left it behind. Dad agreed that Leigh-Anne would appreciate having this relic from his youth and let me regift it. First, I visited a hobby store to buy a clock mechanism and hands. Then, I scoured the web for time-related memorial quotes. I hired a local company to add an engraving to the back on a golden plate that matched the color of the numbers on the front.

"It's beautiful." It was, with an intricate edging along the top that made me wonder what kinds of fancy saws the high school had. The wood grain still shone with his meticulous layers of lacquer.

"Flip it over!"

"A life that touches others goes on forever," she read. "Handcrafted by Aaron Michael Partusch." She flashed me a sad smile, an expression that held a heavy load. "Thank you."

The recipients' reactions were all that I'd hoped. But looking back, I wonder how much of my process was about them. I wonder how much I was tending to my own need to memorialize my brother, to make damn sure he would continue to exist.

Toward the end of the trip, Bob and I visited Aaron's gravesite with Leigh-Anne and his two daughters. My youngest niece sang something cheerful to herself as we quietly followed Leigh-Anne through the patchy grass.

My sister-in-law had warned me that she hadn't yet purchased a gravestone. She seemed torn between the need to buy something affordably basic and the yearning to honor him with the very best. As we walked through the flat cemetery, I imagined a respectable albeit modest marking, maybe something metal and recently scrubbed clean. Something that, while not stone, represented a life well-lived. Instead, when Leigh-Anne stopped walking, I found that the hard ground was marked with a tiny black plastic grave marker mere inches in width. It framed a piece of paper, the top half printed with my brother's name, date of birth, and date of death. The bottom half gave the funeral home's logo and contact information: a full fifty percent of my brother's meager space devoted to promotion. A messy splash of bright blue fell down the top right corner.

"What's that blue?" I asked, already knowing.

"Looks like paint," Bob answered.

I tensed my shoulders, those blue swipes infuriating me. I pictured the carefree groundskeeper stomping through the field in heavy work boots weeks before, a dirty paintbrush swinging in his arm, that booger of enamel flinging through the air and landing on the only thing marking my brother's dead body. Wasn't his life worth more than that? Didn't he deserve more?

I recognized the sensation in my body as anger and, while taking a few deep breaths, mentally thanked it for being there, for demonstrating my devotion to Aaron. Immediately, I felt more aware of the world beyond the grave marker: my husband's warm hand in mine, a cold breeze on bare cheeks, my youngest niece humming. I had been seeing Teresa consistently for a year by then and had grown to trust her. She accepted whatever pain showed up (new, old, or of unknown origin) and taught me how to do the same. The waves of peace I'd come to experience in her office were making their way into my everyday life.

The five of us stood huddled close in the cold while looking down at the skimpy sign. In time, we each cried in our unique ways. Mostly, we were quiet and contained. I saw Bob swipe a couple of tears with a pointer finger. My older niece wrapped her arms around her little sister, who cried the loudest.

"He shouldn't be there," Leigh-Anne said eventually, after all of us had calmed and dried our cheeks. "He's supposed to be up here with us."

My youngest niece looked up. "What, Mommy? What does that mean?"

After a beat, I answered for my sister-in-law. "She's upset that he died. She's saying she wishes he was alive and up here with us."

"Oh."

I was fascinated by how my niece jumped so readily from playfully singing to openly sobbing to nonchalant conversation and back again. How did she do that? It reminded me of what I had learned years before at Mourning Hope, how all kids know how to grieve if we let them.

I looked down at my sweet, freckled niece, whose light brown ponytail with bangs was just like mine had been at that age. Who had lost a parent while in second grade, just as I had. In the middle of that cold, deserted gravesite, watching her navigate her new world, it hit me. It wasn't a sudden light bulb moment. More like, I glanced up and realized I'd been dappled in light all along.

What I saw was that she was born capable, as adept as a river flowing around barriers and forging new paths. We all enter this world knowing how to allow our feelings. My experiences in therapy over the past year were less about learning than they were about unlearning. I was merely moving aside the rocks and fallen tree limbs that interrupted the flow of my natural state of being.

Noticing my stare and mirroring my smile, she inquired, "What?"

"Nothing. I love you."

"Love you too," she offered before side-hugging my waist. I put my arm around her shoulder, gave a squeeze, and relaxed into the support of the earth.

I could remember a time, many years before, when I hadn't yet learned all of these lies about emotional expression. When I found myself thrashing in the choppy waves of my first difficult death, I navigated the waters skillfully with a soft heart.

16 THEN

I had to learn how.

I sat cross-legged on the cold kitchen linoleum, the ruffled edge of my Popples pajamas taut at my knees, petting our yellow lab puppy with both arms. First, I rubbed her smooth belly while she laid down and stuck her four squirming legs in the air. Then, she stood and scooted closer, so I rubbed the top of her soft head and her floppy ears. In response, she gifted me with face licks that made me giggle.

My family let me name her. I picked Cinnamon because her fur reminded me of the sugary cinnamon toast my mom often made me. Our neighbor tried to point out the difference between the spice's warm brown shade and our dog's pale yellow fur, but I didn't much care. I liked the name, and my parents must have too because it stuck.

"I can see your underwear."

I looked up at Aaron who had just walked into the kitchen. "So?"

He reached down and scratched Cinnamon's ears.

Mom, who was watching us and smiling, lifted her hands suddenly with the excitement of a new idea. "Oo! Let's take your picture with the dog!"

"Okay!" Getting my picture taken was fun, especially with Mom's Polaroid.

"Honey, why don't you get on your knees?"

Aaron and I got into position against the kitchen wall, wrangling Cinnamon between us. Copying Aaron, I commanded her to sit, and she eventually plopped her butt down. He pushed gently and repeatedly against her snout, trying to direct her to look forward, while Mom snapped her fingers to get the dog's attention.

"Cimanon, look at Mommy!"

"Okay, smile, you two!"

Satisfied after a few clicks, she set the camera on the kitchen table atop a pile of unopened mail and busied herself with my breakfast dishes.

"Go pick out your clothes. I'll come help you get dressed in a minute, okay?"

Later that afternoon, I was playing in the living room when my dad interrupted. He popped his head inside the front door and yelled for my mom.

Dad often spent his weekends tinkering outside with tools, sanding a thrifted dresser in the garage or changing his sister's oil in the driveway. That day, he'd been working on his own pickup truck.

When she didn't answer, he repeated with an urgency that made the light fuzz on the back of my neck stand at attention. "LuAnne!"

I stared up from my spot on the living room floor, surrounded by strewn children's books I had pulled from the few shelves I could reach. Soon, my mom came running in from the kitchen. "What? What happened?"

"I need you out here."

"Are you okay?"

"It's the dog. Get your purse."

She ran off, returned in a flash with her bulky purse thrust over her skinny right shoulder, and flew out the front door after him.

Later, I learned about the moments leading up to that one. Dad had nearly finished up working that morning. Cinnamon loved going for rides in the bed of his truck, so as usual, he invited her up for a quick neighborhood test drive. On the way home, just a few houses down from ours, she jumped out of the moving vehicle. My dad thought she must have seen a squirrel or a rabbit, and her innate need to retrieve took over.

When my parents returned home from the vet, Aaron and I rushed to the door to get some answers. I didn't see the dog.

"Where's Cimanon?"

Mom glanced at Dad, who was already walking upstairs, then back at us. "Why don't you guys come sit?"

Once the three of us were settled into our chairs at the dining room table, she explained that Cinnamon's hip had been broken, and that surgery would be too expensive and painful. Even if Cinnamon could have surgery, she'd have to wear a wheelchair-like contraption for her hind legs. I'd seen a dog with three legs before, but I'd never seen a dog in a wheelchair. I asked many questions. She said the chair wouldn't work on the snow, so in the winter, we'd have to carry her outside every time she needed to pee. *No biggie*, I thought. Mom could carry the dog outside.

"So, we've decided to put her down."

"What?" Aaron yelled.

"What's that mean?"

I'm not sure what she said, but what I heard was that doctors sometimes kill dogs on purpose, particularly when they were in a lot of pain as Cinnamon was. They make the dog lay down on a table, they give it a shot, and then the dog goes to Heaven like my Great-Grandma did.

"You can't just kill her!" Aaron snapped, throwing his arms up.

I was mad, too. I couldn't understand why she wouldn't just get Cinnamon a special wheelchair. She was my favorite dog in the whole world. But the decision had been made.

The next day, the three of us went to the vet's office to say goodbye. We followed a woman to a massive concrete-floored room in the back where sharp barking filled the air. We walked along a wall of cages, and I slowed to look in each one for Cinnamon. Some of the dogs slept, curled up with their faces away from my view. Others stood tall and barked at me. Some whined sadly, staring at me with pleading eyes. Assuming all of the pets were there for the same reason, I wondered if they knew that they were going to be dead soon.

When we finally arrived at Cinnamon's spot, she was watching us, her tail wagging wildly. She was thrilled to see us and, I suspected, eager to come home. The employee guided her out of the cage on a fat leash. Cinnamon limped our way, dragging one back leg. She didn't look that sick to me. She was moving fine, I noticed, and her wagging tail proved that she was happy. I was not aware of the existence of canine pain killers.

"Look!" I exclaimed to Mom, sure that this revelatory insight would change our dog's destiny. "She's walking! Can we take her home?"

After a pause, Mom answered with downturned eyes, "No, honey. I'm sorry."

My heart sank for the second time in as many days, and I didn't argue. The three of us huddled close, hugging and kissing our dog. We pet her and said goodbye again and again, all three of us crying. I didn't want to go.

"Come on."

I reached up and held Mom's hand. As we walked away, I heard a whine and looked back to see Cinnamon's sad, pleading eyes. *Poor puppy*, I thought. *She knows she doesn't get to see us again.*

In the days and weeks that followed, I returned to life as kids do after great loss. Sometimes I bounced about in joyous play, and sometimes I curled up in pain. I knew she was with God now, but I couldn't be happy for her. I was sad. I wished she was still at home where I could pet her soft belly and stick my head in her neck to get her to lick my face.

"I miss Cimanon," I told Mom through tears one night.

"Oh, honey, I know." She leaned down to see me eye-to-eye and pushed my bangs to one side. "Me too."

"She was a good girl."

"Yes, she was. She was a very good dog. And you remember what I told you? About where she is now?"

I did. "She's in Heaven with Great-Grandma Rerucha and God and Jesus."

"That's right. And it's *so* beautiful there. She's probably in a big, green yard playing all her favorite games with her new friends. Like frisbee, and catch." The mention of play made me smile.

"And chasing her tail!"

"Yeah," she chuckled. "That one is *definitely* chasing her tail."

Mom took me into the safety of her arms, where I lay my head on her shoulder and hugged tight. I was crying and I was laughing and all of it was okay.

I killed Mom.

"How are things going?" Mark asked from behind the L-shaped wooden desk that took up most of the space in his fluorescent-lit office.

Having been at the company about a year and a half, things were going much better. Mark had eventually managed to train me despite juggling endless time-sensitive customer requests and Dan's whims. I was rarely bored, and my work added value.

"Fine," I answered, wondering where the conversation was headed. Even though I was getting positive performance reviews, I was triggered by this meeting. Mark's invitation was more vague than usual: *Quick chat* in the subject line with no additional context provided. He sat stiffly, like he was nervous. What he wanted to tell me couldn't be good.

"How's the workload? You pretty busy?"

"Yeah, it's great. I'm definitely busy, but not *too* busy."

"Good, good. You seem to get along with everybody." He leaned forward and added with a forced grin, "Which isn't always easy at this place."

I smiled for him.

"There is one thing I wanted to talk to you about."

Here it comes.

"I heard from some of the guys about a requirement you wrote up last week."

For a moment, my inner reaction was defensive. *What the hell? Which guys?* I wondered. But as he described the project, I realized that their behavior was justified. My cheeks flushed. It had not been my best work. I had needed help but asking for help wasn't really in my repertoire.

"They told me they had to reach out to the customer themselves with questions."

Ouch. None of the engineers told me that. Talking to the customer was undeniably my job. Making a higher-paid and likely introverted engineer take on such a task was a clear career no-no.

"Now, I gave you the benefit of the doubt. But I went and looked at your work and, I gotta say, they were right. There wasn't enough there."

I nodded, my throat too tight to speak.

"We can't be delivering requirements like that. I need you to be thorough."

A distant, hard-to-access part of my mind recognized that his words were relatively inconsequential. But shame coursed through my body, weighing me down, and it was hard to maintain my composure. I didn't want to be seen as someone who half-assed her work. I hated messing up. My brain felt like a CD skipping, replaying *I did something wrong* over and over. I forced myself to take a breath.

"Of course," I agreed. "You're absolutely right. It won't happen again." *Could we please be done now?*

Back at my desk, I used a visualization tool Teresa had taught me. I imagined setting the feelings, that whole meeting, into a beautiful turquoise ceramic container, trusting that I'd come back to them when the time was right. I had an appointment that very afternoon, which might be the perfect time. But for now, I had to get some work done. And not let anyone see how much a bit of totally reasonable feedback affected me.

Later that day, I settled into a chair in the relative safety of my therapist's office. Teresa sat in a rolling chair across from me. As I told her what happened with my boss, I fidgeted with the tissue in my lap, pinching a thumb and index finger down the length of its center crease. I darted my eyes around the room: to the closed wooden door, briefly into her blue eyes, down at the tissue. I allowed myself to feel what I'd been pushing away since that meeting.

As I wiped away my slowing tears, I said, "I don't understand why I feel so guilty." I was bent over in the chair and almost whining as I spoke, a confused and powerless child.

She wasn't fazed by my overreaction. She simply asked, "When else have you felt this way?"

That was an easy question. I often felt some shade of guilt. We stumbled backwards in time together, my brain dutifully connecting the dots of shame-filled memories, which I briefly verbalized.

Before today's work feedback, guilt reddened my cheeks when I was mean to Bob. I remembered the time I had come inside after a run and snapped when he asked me if I'd planned lunch.

Five and a half years earlier, I felt it in Aaron's kitchen, the first time I visited him in Delaware, when he asked me, *How did I end up here, and you end up there?*

In a rush, my mind flitted through the challenges I had watched Aaron face while I skated easily through life behind him. Getting kicked out of schools before Mom died. Receiving Dad's belt in punishment, a pain I'd gratefully never felt. His many arrests for petty theft and pot paraphernalia. Moving across the country with no money, one credit shy of a high school diploma. Meanwhile, I smoked free pot with my guy-friends in basements, backyard sheds, and cars, not once questioned by police. I got a college scholarship, a new car, and a corporate salary, while Aaron got prison, debt, and more debt.

Why should I have had it so easy?

As memories came up, Teresa guided me to feel without judgment. It was hard, but I was willing. I focused on breathing as big uncomfortable emotions washed through my body.

I remembered the night I didn't come home after Prom, instead crashing at a hotel with my guy friends and too many Smirnoff Ices. I hadn't realized my parents would be making frantic phone calls early the next morning when they found my bedroom empty. How could I have forgotten that parents worry? How could I have been so cruel?

More than a decade before that, in preschool, I once peed in my clothes. I wasn't confident that I could push my tights down and pull them back up by myself, so I figured I could just pee on the floor and no one would know. I sat cross-legged and watched with horror as the wet circle grew underneath me. Two girls pointed and screeched. *Eww! Amanda peed her pants! Amanda peed her pants!* Mom was nice at pick-up time; I didn't get in any trouble like I thought I might.

Then I remembered standing just inches taller than my mom's casket, looking in. I stared at the shiny ivory scarf wrapped around her head to cover her brain surgery scars. I wanted to be closer but was afraid to move, let alone touch her, like Grandma had done.

I snapped open my eyes. I hadn't expected that memory. I didn't want to remember that.

"Isn't it interesting," Teresa said, "how we started with the belief, 'I did something wrong,' and ended up at the memory of your mom's death?"

My eyebrows crinkled. I didn't find it interesting. I found it annoying. Why did this old dead mom thing have to keep butting in, interrupting the progress I was making?

"I'm not seeing a connection." I had only thought of Mom's funeral because I thought of Mom picking me up from preschool, I told myself. Teresa was silent, and I got the sense that she was a few steps ahead of my comprehension. I nudged, "What am I missing?"

She took her time before she spoke. "Many children feel self-blame after a major loss. It's a skillful, normal reaction. It gives them some sense of control in a confusing, frightening, uncontrollable situation."

I had first heard this concept four years earlier, during volunteer training at the family grief center Mourning Hope. I was sure that factoid didn't describe me, though. Emotional transparency aside, my dad had been medically straightforward. He explained my mother's situation to me while she was in the hospital. I always knew it was a brain aneurysm, a physical weakness in her arteries that was bound to rupture.

"Did you ever blame yourself for your mom's death?"

"No," I asserted. "She died of a brain aneurysm." That wouldn't have made any sense. People weren't responsible for aneurysms. I had nothing to feel guilty about.

And yet, I did. I always had.

Since we were at the end of our scheduled time, Teresa skillfully wrapped up our emotional hour in a way that somehow left me feeling fully prepared to rejoin life outside her walls. Although I hadn't made sense of everything, a weight was lifted, and I went about my evening unbothered. The puzzle of that session lingered in the back of my mind but didn't consume me.

A few nights later, I lay awake in bed while Bob snored beside me. I rolled onto my side, my second pillow comfortably situated between my knees, and mentally recapped that strange hour: the shaming thoughts, my intense feelings, Teresa's comment about self-blame in childhood loss. It just didn't add up. I told myself to let it go, that she didn't know what she was talking about. I drifted closer to sleep, hugging the covers tightly to my chest. Then, on the verge of dreamtime, a memory popped into view.

Oh my god. I was suddenly wide awake. Teresa was right.

I remembered the moment on the den couch that awful winter, when my dad described the night that Mom fell sick. I sat next to him that day frozen in terror with the belief that I'd caused her death. Coupled with this memory was a well-worn image, a secondhand replay of Dad's recollections that I had memorized from frequent mental repeats.

The vision was cartoonish: a child's exaggeration born of that single moment on the couch. In my mental movie, it's nighttime, and Dad is in bed sleeping. Mom sneaks quietly toward the bed after staying up late to wrap the rest of my and Aaron's Christmas presents. Standing close to their waterbed, Mom trips on the carpet (on nothing, because she's that tired) and hits her left temple on the corner of the nightstand with so much force that her head bounces after impact. She stands, holding her left palm to her head, her face crinkled in pain, and whispers, *Ow!* Dad grunts a greeting, and Mom slips under the covers. *I'm fine*, she shout-whispers. *Go back to sleep.*

It had been many years since I'd thought about this waking nightmare of my youth. Yet the story was still so familiar it felt factual. And it packed a powerful punch: I was immobilized by the sudden clarity that I was a bad person. That I'd done something unforgivably wrong.

I made her tired. I made her fall. I made her die.

My jaw fell open. How could I have forgotten about these thoughts? And how could something so irrational live on, even into adulthood? It was unsettling to rediscover something I had unconsciously hidden from myself.

Years later I will make more sense of my *magical thinking* experience when reading Hope Edelman's *The AfterGrief: Finding Your Way Along the Long Arc of Loss*. Just like I'd heard before, a kid too young to fully grasp death looks for simple cause-and-effect explanations. These can result in self-blame. What Edelman's research adds is the insight that without revisiting, these stories can persist well beyond childhood. It was my avoidance that let the lie live on.

I had thought about Mom hitting her head hundreds, thousands of times before. But now, I was an adult. And I was present in my body feeling the pain without resistance. I felt the shame. I felt compassion for the little girl who had to carry that burdensome weight for so, so long. I felt compassion for *me*.

The shame soon fizzled out, the storm having been allowed to run its course. My heart rate slowed, and a new insight dropped into my awareness. It explained something that had befuddled me for as long as I could remember.

Maybe *this* was why I felt so overwhelmed by feelings of guilt and shame.

It wasn't just an adult experience. It was *all* of this, bubbling up from childhood, a time when those feelings were too big and scary to face. For the first time, I saw logic in my whirlwind of emotions, and with it came a big sigh of relief. My whole body relaxed, letting go of the fearful story that I was unfixable.

Writing incomplete requirements for my employer didn't make me a bad person.

I wasn't responsible for the quality of my brother's life.

And I didn't kill Mom.

I was innocent. I'd always done the best I could with what I'd had. It's all any of us have ever done.

I rolled over onto my back, stretched out my arms and legs, and smiled up at the ceiling. I was living the formula I'd been hearing about: that when we look at what we're afraid to see, its power diminishes. Greater still, I saw what was possible. I could apply this wisdom to any murky corner of my mind, lightening my load a little more with each honest, compassionate exploration.

I wasn't broken at all—I had just been resisting.

18 THEN

I need my mom.

At seven years old, I sat with my mom at our round dining room table on an easy, air-conditioned summer morning, excited to learn how to sew. It was something I'd seen her do countless times, from patching my dad's socks to the bewildering act of transforming stacks of folded fabric into clothing.

She sandwiched together two pieces of purple fleece that I recognized as Halloween scraps. She'd made me an awesome pink and purple unicorn costume the previous fall. It had a horn made firm from a cereal box base and a long mane of gathered tulle. Mom topped the fuzzy fleece with a cardboard heart about five inches wide that she'd cut out moments before. Then she grabbed her sewing scissors, the big metal ones that were flat on one side. I knew what came next.

"Can I do it?"

"This part's a little hard," she said before looking down at her work and cutting carefully around the template. After the outer pieces of fleece had fallen to the table, she held up the two hearts to show me the result of her innovative technique. I gaped my mouth open in amazement.

"There's two!"

"Mhm," she nodded with a smile, my enthusiasm contagious.

Once she'd realigned the fleece pieces, her nimble fingers expertly passed a needle with its contrasting pink thread down and up, demonstrating the running stitch we'd use to turn the scraps into a tiny pillow.

"This is the most important stitch to learn," she explained seriously, and I felt like an official member of The Big Girls Club. She continued for a few stitches before handing it over. I repeated her motion in larger, less even stitches until she told me I'd done enough.

"I'm not done yet!" I pointed to the gap between where I was and where the stitching began.

"That's fine. Here, I'll show you." She held out her hands, and I reluctantly passed the project over. Concentrating her gaze on her work, she narrated, "I'm tying a knot so it doesn't unravel. There, that should do." Then she stuck two fingers in the small hole we'd left and turned our work-in-progress inside out, hiding the jagged outline of uneven pink dashes.

"Cool!" I admired the transformation. Her trick revealed a clean edge with almost no thread visible.

"Now we get to stuff it." She scooted the open bag of fluffy white polyfill toward me. Once I'd filled it as much as I could, she added a bit more.

"Are we done?"

"Almost. Now, we have to use a different stitch for this little part here. A slip stitch."

"How come?"

"So that it's hidden." She started to demonstrate with the threaded needle, but I was bored.

I whined, "I don't wanna do this anymore." I kicked my feet under the table while Mom completed her work. Finally, she handed the finished piece to me to admire, and I beamed with pride. "I made a pillow!"

"You sure did."

I adored our billowy lopsided heart but would misplace it in the coming days.

Ding! The kitchen timer sounded from the next room.

"Ope! Pie's done." She scooted back from the table, and I followed.

She slipped oven mitts onto her hands, and I peered around her as she opened the door. Inside were a large flat piece of sugared crust and an apple pie, their tops turned golden brown. The buttery smell lined the insides of my nose, making my mouth water. She took the crust out, moving it to the stovetop.

"Can I have some?"

She shook her head. "Mm-mm."

"Just one bite?" I whined. The temptation was hard to bear. Few things were more delicious than Mom's crispy homemade pie crusts.

"This one's for Dad. You can have some pie at Louie and Linda's tonight." It was the fourth of July weekend, and, as usual, we planned to celebrate with our neighbors.

"Fine," I said, adding a pouty face in one last ditch effort to sway her.

She wasn't swayed.

Early that evening, when the sky had just begun to darken, Mom, Linda, and I sat in lawn chairs at the top of Louie and Linda's driveway. The boys were all gathered near the street, lighting wicks I couldn't see. I squeezed my hands over my ears trying to drown out the dreadful explosions, loud sounds whose timings I couldn't predict. My brother, in contrast, grinned ear-to-ear each time something else exploded.

Boom! Another one of the big ones went off, vibrating my chest.

"I don't like those," I said to Mom, hoping she'd make the guys stop.

"Me either," she agreed, though I could tell by her relaxed stance that we didn't feel exactly the same. She looked at the thin gold watch she always wore on her left wrist.

"Ya know," Linda said, "the view from your deck might actually be nicer."

"Ooo, that's an idea." Turning to me, Mom added, "Do you want to go watch from the deck for a bit?"

I stood in agreement and rushed to accompany her back home.

Moments later, we exited the sliding door off of the brown room upstairs and walked onto the deck my dad had built. Wooden seating lined the perimeter. I climbed up and kneeled toward the outside, my hands gripping the back railing. Mom and I watched the fireworks rise into the sky and explode in colorful fountains over the neighborhood. The loud ones weren't as loud from this distance. I was able to relax enough to enjoy the spectacle.

"I like that one," she said after an especially large silver burst. "It looks like diamonds."

"Me too!" I agreed. I often borrowed her identity as my own. Every girl learns how to be a woman by watching her mom.

We sat huddled together until the neighbors' shows ended, until only dissipating smoke clouds could be seen in the night blue sky. Then, I went to bed secure in my awareness that I was loved.

I'm no longer physically with my mother. But I can still access that same well of peace, reminding me that I am and will always be loved.

19 NOW

I'm fixed.

On the way to bed, I paused to gaze out of our living room windows toward the neighboring houses and distant Iowa bluffs. A spontaneous smile emerged. The sky was a winter lavender. The white moon and snow-covered roads, roofs, and yards brightened the black night. I used to make fun of my sister for staring out windows. Now I understood the appeal of this non-activity.

Moments later, with my teeth clean and my contacts in their case for the night, I reached under the sink and grabbed my gratitude journal. I loved that squat little book, with one five-section page for each date of the year. At night I would turn to the correct page, scribble the year by the first open section, and add a few specific phrases about what I was grateful for from the past twenty-four hours.

This habit was inspired by one of the many self-help books I'd read. It was in one such book, a fun exercise-filled read by Martha Beck about finding your right life, that I first heard of the field of life coaching. My body had buzzed with excitement. *That would be the* perfect *career for me,* I realized.

The venture of squeezing more joy out of life thrilled me. Every new year, I spent hours defining my annual goals and collaging my vision. Bored by superficial chit chat, I asked people about their dreams when hovering around party plates of hummus. I also had a growing ability to compassionately challenge nonsense, a core skill of a quality coach. My bluntness had softened over the past few years as my values shifted, kindness now ranking as high as honesty. I encouraged my team members to set more inspiring goals. To Bob's weeknight complaint that he *didn't accomplish anything all day,* I might respond with, *Did you make anyone smile?*

I was so convinced about this direction that I ordered the inch-thick textbook, *Becoming a Professional Life Coach,* from Amazon. When it was delivered in its too-big cardboard box, I drank up the first few pages. Then, overwhelmed by how doable the authors made this alternative life sound, I carried it to my shelf, deflated. I sat it atop *Fung Shui Your Life,* an oversized book that had stayed through several moves thanks to containing both interior design tips that appealed to my early-twenties self and mindfulness lessons that felt increasingly relevant a decade later.

I quit my stressful *thick-skin* job the previous summer, after four years there. At the time, I wasn't ready to take on the risk of entrepreneurship in the entirely new-to-me industry of coaching. Instead, willing only to brave a new employer, I secured a leadership role at a growing tech startup. Meanwhile, the coaching textbook gradually made its way to the bottom of the stack, becoming easier and easier to ignore.

Leaning against the bathroom counter, I looked up at the ceiling and mentally skimmed through the preceding workday with a goal to gather evidence of genuine gratitude. It wasn't difficult. I was now seven months into my new job and loved it. My days were fast-paced and fun. My coworkers were some of the kindest, most creative folks I'd ever worked with. Most had side projects: a freelance graphic design business, a photography project to empower women, a traveling soup kitchen. Especially mind-blowing to me was that no one expected them to hide these interests. We were not only allowed but encouraged to show up as our full selves. It was written right into the company values: *We are weird.*

With some ideas of what to add to my journal, I reached for my phone, plugged into the charger beside the sink, to check the date. The screen read *January 9.* My eyebrows lifted in surprise. The next day would be January tenth, the anniversary of my mother's death. Funny that I could forget, given how irritable I'd been feeling. Earlier that night, I had yanked hard on Keira's leash and shouted *Heel!* through gritted teeth. I imagined myself snapping like that at work but quickly shrugged off the fear. It was going to be a busy day; I'd be too distracted to think about Mom.

The next morning at the office I stood at my white electric standing desk, focusing my eyes on the large monitor and typing away at my keyboard. I was preparing for a company-wide presentation I was scheduled to give right after lunch. Off to my right, two of my coworkers had jumped into a loud venting session about the sales team again.

"It's not even built yet! Why would they sell it?"

Didn't they see me trying to get actual work done? With great animation, I swooped my arm toward the headphones on my desk, grabbed my laptop, and stormed as loudly as I could over to the quietest corner on the floor. Sitting stiffly on the sofa, I let loud music drown out the people around me and refocused on my presentation prep.

At lunch, anger boiled below my neutral appearance. I sat at a small round table with a few engineers, one of them droning on about his latest algorithmic challenge. I wondered how he could possibly think I found his one-sided conversation interesting. My upper body was tense, and I wanted to ball my hands into fists. I noticed I held back tears and wondered if it was because of the date. I wasn't thinking about my mom, though. Not consciously. What I was thinking about was the fact that it was Demo Day, and in twenty minutes I would have to present to the entire company.

I could *not* be teary-eyed in front of seventy people.

I took a breath, and with it came a slight release of frustration in the form of clarity.

Of course it's the date. This happens every year. I need to ask for help.

I spotted a nearby table of women I knew well. Could I open up to them, I wondered?

I thought back to the group I'd opened up to several months before at my neighborhood yoga studio. Its owner created a community in which I felt safe. Unlike other yoga teachers I'd encountered, she gave me permission to ignore her instructions in favor of my body's guidance. After classes, we sipped herbal tea together and talked about our lives' ups and downs. When I confessed that some asanas made me feel like crying, an experience I called *weird*, they reclassified it as *normal*.

After a handful of visits, I let myself full-on sob during pigeon pose. A position known for its power to release emotions, it made me think of my brother and mom. Lying on my mat with one knee angled outward, I felt like Little Mandy again, crying silently under my covers. I was a grown woman doing yoga on Tenth Street. And I was a scared child on Vinton Street who missed her mommy. But I wasn't alone anymore. And no one— not even me—was trying to fix it.

What if that were possible here, too, at this office where I typically demanded of myself a polished and confident demeanor?

Though my coworker was mid-sentence and making eye contact, as if his convoluted explication was for me, I slinked off with a smile and a nod. After taking a seat, I picked my nails under the table while waiting for a partial pause in the conversation. The women seated opposite me glanced over briefly and smiled, as if to invite dialogue. They must have sensed something was up because one by one each quieted.

"I need some support," I said.

Melanie from the People team asked with genuine concern, her eyes on mine, "What's going on?"

I explained what January tenth meant to me. How it didn't matter that it was twenty-five years ago. "I know it seems crazy, but I still get sad about it."

"What? That's not crazy, Mandy."

"Yeah, that sounds *awful*. I can't imagine losing my mom."

"It makes me want to cry just *thinking* about what would happen to my daughter if I died." Kaitlin shook her head, and I thought back to the crisp autumn evening when I met her smiling, chubby-cheeked three-year-old at a company cookout.

While these women translated the shock of my share into painful personal *what ifs*, my sympathy remained self-directed. I felt a little calmer since I'd stated my pain and been affirmed, but not calm enough to get up and present.

"You know," Kaitlin shared from the end of the table, "my grandma died when my mom was real young."

"Really?" someone replied.

The conversation around us was loud, as usual. I looked at Kaitlin, trying to shift fully into listening mode and filter everything else out. It was harder than usual given my emotional state.

"Yeah. She was just a teenager I think. It's still really hard for my mom."

The conversation moved on while my stressed-out brain tried to process what she'd said. Like me, Kaitlin's mom was still grieving decades later. I absorbed this detail, and then I nodded along with the table. I directed eye contact with the table. I expressed concern with the table.

Liz, sitting to my right, turned to me and asked, "Do you have any siblings?"

Immediately my eyes were wet, and I held my breath to keep the lump from traveling up my throat. I swallowed, chuckled like my dad would, and said, "Man, I'm really sad!" I gave the table the Cliff's Notes version of my brother's death. They listened intently, and my heart ached and rejoiced all at once.

"What else can we do for you?" Melanie asked. "Can I give you a hug?"

I grinned, sheepish. I felt childlike: hesitant to admit my vulnerability yet eager for the simple comfort of an embrace.

She defended, "I'm a big hugger."

"Okay, sure." As she squeezed me, I joked nervously, "Wow! That's a real hug!"

She hung on. After a few seconds, the interaction nearing awkward proportions, I felt my body release with a big sigh of breath. My shoulders dropped, and I sank into the embrace, finally calm.

"There it is!" Melanie said, smiling and stepping back, satisfied.

I hadn't realized I needed that. The experience was so different from my hardest days some four years before. Back then, I'd suppress my sadness at the office and still be unable to cry once I was home alone in bed, having blocked my husband's compassionate attempts to connect. Maybe I didn't have to fight against my feelings anymore. Maybe I could drop my strict self-expectations and simply trust myself.

A few minutes before the presentation was scheduled to begin, I stepped to the front of the room with a warm grin, feeling confident. As I progressed through the slides touting the work our team had accomplished, I was focused. My coworkers were always a great audience, but that day I could have sworn that they were laughing and clapping even more than usual.

In the evening, I headed to bed a bit early, feeling joyful but spent: a day fully lived. As usual, I opened up my gratitude journal.

It was fun to read through what I had written on today's date but in past years. To see at a glance how much had changed, and how much hadn't. I tended to skip the practice only when I was feeling too sad to write, but those missed days had become infrequent.

I was surprised to see that the page for *January 10* was completely blank. For the three or four years I'd had the habit, this was the first January tenth that I'd felt well enough at bedtime to write. I felt especially grateful for my emotional skills: for the joy of knowing what it feels like to ask for and receive a little help.

I scribbled, *A ride to work from Bob. Yummy salad at lunch. Supportive coworkers and my willingness to ask for help when I was sad.*

I cozied up on the couch with the heavy hardback *Becoming a Professional Life Coach,* feeling inspired to find content ideas for my new website. Since I worked at a tech company that hosted websites, I had created one myself to better understand the process. Of course, I was also baby stepping toward my simmering dream to become a life coach, but that angle didn't feel safe to announce. Still, when I showed it to a few coworkers, they were all so damn supportive. They oohed and aahed at the teal and gold theme I'd selected and shared what they knew about search engine optimization. The CEO even smiled at the alliteration of my URL. *Coach Kubicek,* he'd read aloud. *I like that.*

I lifted my feet onto the coffee table and crossed my legs at the ankles. Settling into the cushions behind me, I turned to Chapter One and quickly became engrossed by the well-organized sections and their reflective exercises.

A good coach will *walk the talk*, the authors wrote. So I drew my own *Wheel of Life*, a circle with wedges for each life area. Then I colored each wedge in the spot that aligned with my current level of satisfaction: toward the circle's center for low satisfaction, toward the outer edge for high.

When complete, I held my notebook at arm's length and looked at the wheel scribbled on the page. The wedges shaded along the outside edge included personal growth, career, and money. With romance, the middle area was shaded. I sighed at this acknowledgement on paper of what I'd been reluctant to admit to myself. Our marriage was just okay.

Ever since Bob and I had started dating in college, people said things like, *You two are just the perfect couple!* Single middle-aged women especially swooned over our hand-holding. I'd always wondered what they were thinking when they said these semi-ridiculous things. Yeah, we liked each other, but didn't most people who chose to spend their lives together? Did they think we never argued? Did they imagine our after-dinner dishwashing was like a Dick Van Dyke special, all smiles and music and dancing?

Well, sometimes it was. But more synth-pop Robyn than *Chim Chim Cher-ee.*

Regardless, this was part of my identity: haver of the perfect marriage. The truth was, I hadn't felt that close to Bob lately. Yes, as I worked through my own backlog of unmet needs, I was better able to respond to his. I hugged him more often, told him how I really felt, and got better at ignoring the fearful stories spinning in my head that turned his neutral words into weapons. But we were both wrapped up in our jobs. We got home tired and opted to watch TV during dinner instead of talking. I liked to go to bed earlier than he did, and we'd let our schedules drift apart.

That evening, I initiated a conversation.

"So, I was doing this exercise in my coaching book." I waited for him to read the text notification that popped up on his watch. "There's something I want to talk to you about." When he adjusted his position on the couch, I knew I had his full attention. My stomach rolled in nerves, uncertain how he'd react: defensive, disinterested, dismissive? "I feel kind of... distant from you lately." My shoulders were up to my ears.

He smiled slightly. "Me too."

I sighed a breath of relief. "You have?"

"Yeah. It's just… work's been busy. And I want to stay up late, but I know it's not good."

"I'd really like to spend more time together. Like, quality time. Not just sitting on the couch and watching stupid videos."

"Freddie Mercury isn't stupid," he replied with a smirk, referencing a concert video he'd been playing on repeat. My shoulders relaxed in response to his playfulness. We agreed to go to bed at the same time most nights and to pre-schedule a weekly date night.

"Okay," I said as we settled on Thursdays, "but going out to dinner can't count as a date."

He nodded. "Yeah. Let's say, at least two activities for it to count."

"Deal."

We stuck to our commitment.

Sitting at a round banquet table in a massive hotel meeting room with more than a hundred other coaches-in-training, I half-listened to the teachers on stage answering audience questions. My body buzzed with the excitement of being with so many like-minded new friends at this oceanside meet-and-greet event near San Luis Obispo, California.

Several months before, after realizing my single textbook wasn't enough to prepare me for a coaching career, I had signed up for an eight-month remote training program with Martha Beck. At first, my mind went on overdrive analyzing the pros and cons of the investment. How could I spend all of that money, I told myself, when I already had an enjoyable job and a predictable salary? At the same time, I felt shrunken when I imagined *not* doing it. The Sunday morning when I finally signed up, I rushed into the bedroom where Bob was still in bed, just waking up. *Guess what?* I asked as I lay down beside him. *What?* he replied, a grin appearing, my joy infectious. I rolled onto my back and thrust my pelvis in the air a few times to bounce the bed like a kid on Christmas morning. I leaned in close to his face and whispered into his ear. *I just spent so much money!*

I had no regrets. I loved the course materials, my classmates, and the teachers. Beck taught that my thoughts were the cause of my feelings, my feelings drove my actions, and those actions, then, caused my situation. This felt consistent with what I'd experienced in Teresa's office. I'd spent most of my life focused on changing what I was doing, which only got me so far. The juicy stuff came with questioning what I believed and allowing myself to feel.

Coach training seemed to take my therapy learnings to a new level. It was as if, when I was drowning, therapy taught me to tread water. Then coaching propelled me forward in the sea. I didn't stop feeling my unpleasant feelings, as I once hoped would be the case. Rather, I learned to stay afloat even when my body surged with them. I began to swim with ease, instead of constantly demanding momentum.

Plus, the trip kind of felt like magic.

A decade before, when I was debating what to do after college, I made a spreadsheet of potential cities to live in. I pulled in data like crime rates, cost of living, number of sunny days per year, and access to top grad schools. Though I had never been there, San Luis Obispo ranked number one on this list. And here was this city popping into my awareness again.

As a woman on stage demonstrated a coaching tool by helping a standing audience member decide how to navigate a conflict with her teenage daughter, my mind ruminated on my own unmade decision. All weekend I kept hearing about a one-day equus coaching workshop (as in, horses helping to coach humans) being held the day after this event. It sounded like great fun to spend the day outside with coaches I admired, interacting with horses in a more intimate way than I'd experienced.

Something occurred to me then. The only reason I hadn't signed up for the workshop was because I was afraid to spend the money on myself. And since I technically had the money, that wasn't a great reason.

I rushed up to the stage as soon as the session concluded. "Excuse me?" I asked, heart racing. "Is it still possible to sign up for the equus coaching tomorrow?"

I bought one of the last open spots.

The next morning, I squinted under the early sun and breathed in the grounding scents of fresh air, grass, and manure. Twenty or so of us self-improvement junkies filled haystacks, plastic lawn chairs, and picnic tables. We were surrounded by horses in barn stalls, horses in outdoor rings, and a collie running in circles. I came with a straightforward purpose: to reduce my work-related stress and anxiety. I'd been given more strategic responsibility than I'd had in other roles, and my expectations for myself exceeded reality. But when it was time to share my intentions with the group, I was caught off guard by sudden tears.

"I don't know why, but what's coming up for me is losing my mom." After Aaron died, I found myself thinking often about her. But she hadn't been on my mind much lately. "She died, like, twenty-six years ago... So," I sighed. "I guess my intention is to be present with this grief."

I wasn't the only one moved to tears. There were stories of feeling insignificant. Of suppressing all visible emotions. One woman, fidgeting with her long dirty blonde hair, said she had always been a horse person. She competed with them as a child and owned them as an adult. Big tears fell down her prominent cheekbones, and she added, "I haven't spent time with any horses since my husband died four years ago."

Once each of us had a chance to speak, the facilitators introduced us to the concept of equus coaching. They explained that despite their size, horses are prey animals who need to be highly alert. When a person's actions aren't aligned with their true feelings, the horse is on guard. And because horses seek connection, even with us humans, they'll provide feedback on how authentically we're showing up in the ring.

As we split into groups, one with each human coach, I was drawn to Dixie, a small quiet woman whose thick hair fell past the small of her back. She struck me as nurturing. When it was my turn for one-on-one time with a horse, Dixie asked me how I was feeling. Outside the ring, we were surrounded by potential distractions. Eight or nine people chatted in chairs nearby, horses trotted around rings, and the ranch staff and their many dogs walked up and down the dirt road beside us. Yet I felt her full attention focused on me.

Holding back tears, I told her, "I'm afraid to cry."

"Why?"

I searched inside myself for the answer. "I'm afraid that if I start crying, I might not stop." As soon as I acknowledged this fear aloud, I realized it wasn't true. The relief was so complete that I immediately began crying. It felt utterly satisfying. I told Dixie how, at seven years old, I wasn't able to let this grief out. How I wanted to die then. Her own mother had passed just days before, a fact that I'd overheard in conversation. Now, with the mention of my loss, I felt compelled to acknowledge hers.

"I'm sorry about your mom."

"Thank you. What most people don't know," she confided, "is that my father died when I was seven." She also happened to have a daughter named Mandy. She offered an embrace, which I eagerly accepted. As I pulled back from our big hug, a weight lifted, a classmate handed me a tissue. I wiped my eyes and blew my nose. My breathing steadied.

I was ready to have some fun.

First, I stood in the middle of the ring holding a rolled-up long line in my right hand, the metal end in my left. With me was a beautiful chestnut horse named Panache. He had a white line down his face and a white spot on his muzzle. With a smile, I jiggled the line and moved around the ring, and Panache trotted along to my lead. I laughed, overjoyed that he was following me.

Suddenly, the horse stopped, turned directly toward me, and stared. I froze in place with fear, my breath caught in my throat.

Head-on, he seemed much bigger than I had realized. I didn't like that I didn't know what he was thinking. He seemed angry at me. Was he going to charge me?

"What's coming up for you?" Dixie asked calmly from beyond the metal enclosure. "Do you want me to come in with you?"

I nodded. With Dixie beside me, I felt safe again. Although she'd only met this horse that weekend, I'd seen her effortlessly guide him in circles in demonstration before we began. Now, Dixie and I talked about what I was thinking and feeling. She helped me connect my experience with this horse with the patterns of my childhood: being concerned about what the adults around me thought and felt, and changing or suppressing myself in response. We talked about being playful.

"If your mom was here, what would you want to do with her?"

"I don't know."

"How could you be playful with the horse?"

I was stumped. "I guess... Well, what I really want to do is pet him."

I stood in the middle of the ring, my running shoes sinking half an inch into muddy sand, and rubbed the soft reddish-brown hair on his strong neck. Like Dixie, Panache was fully present. He wasn't planning his next move or judging what I'd just said. (He was a horse, after all.) I supposed he felt safe next to me because my actions were consistent with my true feelings. Finally, I wasn't a grieving child pretending to be okay for the sake of the adults around me. How I felt and how I let myself be was one and the same.

And that's a place I had needed to be for a long time.

While I pet him, Panache stood still and slowly wrapped his head behind mine, his muzzle on my back: a horse hug. My chest warmed with gratitude. From within this animal embrace, I felt a full-body tingle of connection.

I realized something in that ring with my coaches, one two-legged and one four-legged. I couldn't sit with Mom at our old dining room table and hand stitch her fabric scraps into heart pillows, or lay next to her on my bed and listen to her voice become Papa Bear, then Mama Bear, and back again as she flipped through a *Berenstain Bears* book. But it *was* within my power to create that same feeling state. To experience connectedness.

The afternoon included group work with the horses. In a larger arena set up with different obstacles (a dozen traffic cones, three barrels, a couple of logs) we formed a team of four people and one horse. Our assignment was to collectively guide the horse through the obstacle course. It seemed simple until we heard the twist: no talking.

"So," the lead coach asked, "what is everyone's intention for the exercise?"

I shared that I wanted to have fun instead of needing to *do* something, to achieve a goal, to meet the high expectations I constantly set for myself.

In the arena our team was in sync, easily guiding the black horse behind three orange cones. He stopped just short of the finish line, looking terrified of the wooden log lying across his path. Nearly laughing, I shook the long line in my right hand, silently urging him to lift his front right hoof over the log. When he cleared it, I thrust my arms into the air, silently cheering him to the finish.

Back in the stands beside the arena, the lead coach asked the observing group, "What did you notice?"

"Mandy was clearly having fun!"

"Yeah, Mandy, you actually *look* different than you did this morning."

"I agree," added another. "You look completely different. Softer, maybe?"

Once, I saw a series of before and after photos online that showed attendees of a month-long meditation retreat. Their faces were wholly transformed, from tense, alert, and pulled taut, to loose, relaxed, and rounded. I knew a physical shift was possible, but this had only been a few hours. I felt great; I felt free. But I couldn't look that different, could I? I decided they must have been imagining it, seeing what they wanted to see. People love feeling like they've witnessed a transformation.

Still, before leaving the farm in the shuttle van, I snuck off to the narrow restroom in the back of one of the barns to peek in a mirror just in case.

My reflection amazed me. Though it was obvious there had been a change, it was hard to put my finger on what that contrast was exactly. It was almost like seeing an absence of features. I must have had my ears pulled back and my eyebrows lifted unconsciously, stretching the skin tight. Creating angles and extraneous lines. The face I saw now was relaxed, though not droopy—like everything was where it was designed to be. What I saw in the mirror matched how I felt: at home. I was present in my body, grounded to the soil beneath my feet, and at peace with every aspect of who I was. Though I was surprised to be mourning my mother that day, I didn't categorize it as a problem.

I had seen how to work *with* my feelings instead of fighting against them. That didn't mean getting rid of the metaphorical box that helped me survive my childhood. But when I tucked my needs inside, it was intentional. I honored my tenderness in moments of upset. I trusted when a memory emerged from the box and asked for my attention. And I had proven to myself that I was willing to listen.

Maybe we aren't meant to realize some satisfying Marie Kondō tidied-up ideal, a decluttering of the emotional self that can be checked off of a to-do list. Maybe a lifetime isn't long enough to free all of the neglected needs we've stuffed inside just to get by. And yet, isn't the journey worth it? That day, I was shown an energizing truth that I'd been waiting decades to learn:

When I allow myself to grieve, I make space for play. And from that state of playfulness, everything I want becomes accessible. I feel the kind of healthful peace that smooths the lines on my face, buoyant joy that delights in the everyday, and, above all, a love unfettered by shame or resentment.

EPILOGUE

I want to be over it.

"Mind if I do headphones?" Bob asked one evening as we carried our dirty plates to the kitchen. He liked how listening to an entertaining audiobook made doing the dishes not only tolerable but enjoyable.

"No. Actually, is it cool if I call my dad instead of helping? It's been a few weeks."

"Good idea."

Over the past several months, I had turned to the tools I learned in life coach training, particularly those taught by Byron Katie, with an intention to forgive my father. It had been four years since he shared something that shifted my perspective about our relationship.

We were standing together against the wall of a packed room at yet another family visitation. My aunt's partner had died unexpectedly in his sleep due to an undiagnosed heart condition. He was the same age as my dad, who had already suffered one heart attack. That evening, I felt an urgency for us to reconcile. *I was thinking*, I said, *maybe we should talk more often.* I was certain he'd agree that talking every few months wasn't ideal. I *don't know about that,* he replied. *Maybe you could not be so upset when we talk.* Convinced that I hid my emotions well, I was so shocked that I couldn't say anything more.

Later, I realized he was right. When I dialed my dad's number, I was usually thinking, *He never calls because he doesn't care about me.* Then I translated his go-to greeting, *You're alive!* into an accusation. I turned his enthusiastic storytelling and lack of questions into, *He doesn't love me.* My behavior reflected how upset I felt. At best, I half-listened to his long-winded stories. I feigned concern rather than judgment when I asked about his diet. I rolled my eyes in jealous frustration as he recounted the household repairs he completed for Melissa. Without fail, I rushed to get off the phone.

Gradually, I was learning that the source of my pain wasn't his behavior so much as how I interpreted it. After diligent daily application of Katie's self-reflection techniques, my stressful stories began to drop away like loose baby teeth that had served their purpose. In their place strange new holes appeared. I explored the disquieting spaciousness with my tongue until they filled themselves up with something sturdy and new:

What I have to say matters.

I didn't mess up.

I'm lovable.

"Hi, Dad!" I greeted him. "Just calling to catch up. You in the middle of anything?"

"No, no, not all," he answered before launching into family updates. He told me about Melissa, Cheri, and their aging Pomeranian. His voice lit up when he got to Melissa's son.

"You should hear some of the things he says!"

I leaned back on the couch with my legs up on the coffee table and held my cell phone to my ear. "What do you mean?" I asked, my curiosity piqued.

"Butt-this, butt-that. He's a riot. He is. I just don't understand why everything has to be about *butts.*"

"Well, he *is* a nine-year-old boy."

"I guess. So, what's new? You gonna get a job yet?"

I grinned, thinking how strange my professional decisions must seem to a man who had two employers for the bulk of his fifty-year career. A couple of years before, about a month after my thirty-fourth birthday, I left my enjoyable tech job to follow my entrepreneurial dreams.

Since a part of me always believed I wouldn't outlive my mother, I had anticipated a difficult thirty-fifth birthday. I was caught off-guard by a depressive episode that hit me the winter before that major milestone. On the worst morning, I spent an hour loudly sobbing at the edge of my bed, trying to will myself to stop so I could go be a productive employee. I wasn't planning to quit. I did want to write and run a coaching business, but not yet. However, the moment I made the decision, peace poured through my veins. In Hope Edelman's brilliant bestseller *Motherless Daughters: The Legacy of Loss*, she describes us as being determined to achieve our ambitious goals before we reach the age at which our mothers died. This is what I believe my body was shouting at me. I'm grateful I listened.

"No way," I answered. "You know how much I hate being told what to do."

Some thirty minutes later, I was smiling as we ended our call.

"How's your dad?" Bob asked from the hall, pulling a headphone from one ear.

"He's great!" I calmly recapped the family news.

That moment between Bob and I was a scene that had played out countless times before. Together, we'd prepare for me to call my parent. I'd have the phone call. Then, we'd rehash the phone call. I'd vent about how my dad never listens, or that Cheri asks too much of me. I might admit aloud to feeling hurt or frustrated, or else my body language would give me away. Bob would wrap his arms around me and shower me with words of affirmation like, *You're a good daughter.*

That day, I noticed how much the pattern had changed. It wasn't merely that my dad and I were talking twice a month. I got off the phone with him and felt energized.

I still sometimes felt triggered by something he'd say or not say. I had barely begun to examine my resentment toward Cheri or my distant relationship with Melissa. But I knew how to make progress, and I had evidence of success. The most freeing part was that no one else had to change a thing.

I've improved my relationship with my mother, too. For a long time, I had few vivid positive memories with her. Maybe this was an early coping mechanism to shield me from the pain of remembering what I'd lost. Maybe I was so attached to the *I'm not lovable* story that my brain edited out the times when I felt most loved. All I know is that during my work with Teresa, after two decades of wishing I could remember more, I did. The image of a golden treasure chest came to mind in one of our sessions, its lid hinged open, emitting beams of bright light. Inside were sparkling oversized sapphires, rubies, and emeralds, each a loving and joyful memory waiting to be unearthed. I wrote them into this book.

I'm almost forty now. Despite being five years older than Mom ever made it, I don't picture her that young. I see her aging alongside me, always a generation ahead in wisdom. Plus, since it's my imagination, I choose to give her a dash of afterlife perfection. For instance, she has never guilt-tripped me about not giving her grandchildren, which, as a Catholic mom, she *totally* would have.

I see Aaron similarly lightened by the transition, his rebellious personality intact but unburdened. I think of him and smile when my neighborhood cracks and pops for several hazy weekends in the summer, teenagers lighting firecrackers in the streets. I got my first tattoo shortly after he died, a geometric tree that symbolizes growth. An *A* for Aaron and an *L* for LuAnne are penned into the triangular foliage between my shoulder blades. I imagine he'd be impressed and supportive as I dream up my next design.

I also like to think that our mom and my other play-deprived women ancestors get to play now through me. Mom hangs out when I travel to new places: the stunning fjords of New Zealand, an ultramarathon high in the Colorado Rockies, or a Mexican beach town for Christmas with my in-laws. And, in a way, she can still offer me guidance. When I notice my shriveled succulents, I apologize to the sky for not inheriting her green thumb. Then I search the web for tips. She hovers nearby as I write and rewrite this story, suggesting sentences.

Sometimes, I intentionally seek out contexts that invite my mom in, like baking. Chocolate-chip cookies are my favorite dessert. I omit the eggs and sub in a cholesterol-free vegan butter that didn't exist in her lifetime. When I make a batch, she's in my kitchen, too, excited for our upcoming sugar high. I stand in front of my kitchen countertop savoring a bite of raw dough and am transported in time. The act reminds me of Mom, Aaron, and I huddled beside the sink on Vinton Street, licking a spatula or mixer attachment. In this way, I recreate the sensation that filled me up at my brother's motorcycle crash site.

I don't want closure. I don't want to be over it. I want to feel connected to the people I love, whether they're living or not.

Would you write a review?

Honest online reviews make a big difference in whether books are discovered and read. In about two minutes, you can help others find and choose this memoir by leaving a review on Amazon or your favorite book review website.

Thank you for helping my work connect with the people who are looking for it.

Acknowledgements

Thank you, Bob, for endless encouragement, impeccable feedback, and supporting my work despite your discomfort with the jack-off scene.

Thank you, Dad and Cheri, for letting me write publicly about our private lives together.

Thank you to my writing coach and editor, Malar Ganapathiappan, for helping me rediscover the fun of writing, structure this book, and move forward despite the emotional ups and downs of memoir.

Thank you to every writers' group participant, including conscious Genevieve Williams, generous Sarah Abdouch, astute Hannah Spraul (a.k.a. Jackary Salem), luminous Karrie Zai, artistic Evelyn Render Katz, learner Larry Fangman, passionate David Barg, supportive Kristin Knisley, and those of you whose names I don't know. Your consistent participation, insightful suggestions, and generous warm-fuzzies helped bring this book to life in a very big way.

Thank you to innovative Hope Edelman and my classmates compassionate Angela Schellenberg, creative Beth Klaisner, comical Dixie Perkinson, feminist Laura Joyce-Hubbard, nurturing Janna Northrup, daring Julie Klein, bright Joy Newcom, and warmhearted Margie Schwaninger for our powerful memoir workshop. Your teaching, experience sharing, feedback, and encouragement helped make my manuscript shine.

Thank you to playful Erica Trabold, warm Alexandra Franzen, wise Lindsey Smith, and no-bullshit Cassie Mannes Murray for teaching me about book publishing and publicity.

Thanks to all of my ARC readers who helped me close this book's remaining gaps and feel confident enough to launch.

Thank you to my early cheerleaders: Jessica Hendry Nelson, editor of my shitty first draft; Pat, a technical writer at the *thick skin* job; and every teacher and friend who ever praised a poem, short story, or sentence I'd written.

Thank you to the countless folks in my life who have encouraged this project. Your words of affirmation, smiling eyes, and listening ears mattered.

Every person in my life—whether written about or not—helped me learn the lessons I've attempted to put in these pages. Thank you all.

And thank *you* for reading.

Reflection questions

Consider the following questions for a group discussion or individual reflection.

1. How did the title, *I Killed Mom and Other Lies*, shape your expectations or interpretation of the book?

2. Who were your favorite characters, and why? Do they remind you of anyone in your life?

3. In the prologue, Mandy Kubicek provides the following conclusion from *Never the Same: Coming to Terms with the Death of a Parent* by Donna Schuurman: "two foundational actions one can take to address a parent's death are to feel one's emotions and share them with others." She also writes that "loss is more than death: it's a geographic move, an ended relationship, an identity gone." What have you lost? What would you like to share with others about your most painful losses?

4. What does the porcelain figurine on the cover represent to you?

5. Consider the job Kubicek begins in Chapter 1 which requires "thick skin." Have you ever hid an emotional reaction at work? What expectations or beliefs (from our culture, the workplace, or yourself) might have contributed to that choice?

6. Kubicek mentions a variety of emotional regulation tools she used, such as reading an affirmation, visualizing a container to temporarily hold feelings, running, keeping a gratitude journal, and questioning the stories she told herself. What helps you respond to unpleasant emotional experiences?

7. What did you learn about early childhood parent loss from reading this story?

8. In the closing paragraph of the final chapter, Kubicek writes, "When I allow myself to grieve, I make space for play. And from that state of playfulness, everything I want becomes accessible." Do you mostly agree or disagree with this statement? Why?

9. In the epilogue, Kubicek writes about the ritual of baking cookies to remember her loved ones: "I stand in front of my kitchen countertop savoring a bite of raw dough and am transported in time." What memorial rituals do you practice, or would you like to start? (Check out the website and app *Be Ceremonial* for ideas.)

10. If you could only remember one thing from this memoir, what would you want it to be?

Author bio

Mandy Kubicek is a software product manager, Certified Life Coach, and author of *My Tender Loving Self-Care Journal: The Workbook that Makes Self-Care Easy.*

A lifelong learner and navel-gazer, Mandy has trained with Martha Beck (aka Oprah's life coach) and Byron Katie. She holds an MBA from Washington University in St. Louis and a BS from the University of Nebraska–Lincoln. She's been writing creative nonfiction since the classroom gossip column she started on a chalkboard during indoor recess.

Known for her insightful questions and giant salads, Mandy lives in Omaha, Nebraska. Learn more at coachkubicek.com.

Printed in the USA
CPSIA information can be obtained
at www.ICGtesting.com
JSHW081031190923
48555JS00001B/4

9 781736 285411